YOUTH DEVELOPMENT IN FOOTBALL

The identification and development of talented young players has become a central concern of football clubs at all levels of the professional game, as well as for national and international governing bodies. This is the first book to offer a comprehensive survey and assessment of youth development programmes in football around the world, to highlight best practice and to offer clear recommendations for improvement.

The book draws on original, in-depth research at eight elite professional football clubs, including Barcelona, Ajax and Bayern Munich, as well as the French national football academy at Clairefontaine. It adopts a multidisciplinary approach, including psychology, coaching and management studies, and covers every key topic from organisational structures to talent recruitment and performance analysis to player education and welfare. Written by two authors with extensive experience in English professional football, including five Premier League clubs, this book is important reading for any student, researcher, coach, administrator or academy director with an interest in football, youth sport, sports development, sports coaching or sport management.

Mark Nesti is Reader in Sport Psychology at Liverpool John Moores University where he is also head of the MSc programme in Sport Psychology. His current research interests are focused on identity, meaning and critical moments in sport. Mark was formerly the counselling sport psychologist to the first team at Bolton Wanderers (2003–7), Newcastle United FC (2007–8) and Hull City AFC (2008–10) in the Premier League.

Chris Sulley is Head of Coaching (5–13) at the Everton FC Academy where his focus is on developing the coaching skills and competencies congruent with the club's playing and coaching philosophy. Chris is a former professional footballer, starting his career in a very successful youth development programme at Chelsea (1972–81) before moving on to Bournemouth (1981–6), Dundee United (1986–7), Blackburn Rovers (1987–92), Port Vale (1992–3) and Preston North End (1993–5).

YOUTH DEVELOPMENT IN FOOTBALL

Lessons from the world's best academies

Mark Nesti and Chris Sulley

Routledge
Taylor & Francis Group

LONDON AND NEW YORK

First published 2015
by Routledge
2 Park Square, Milton Park, Abingdon, Oxon OX14 4RN

and by Routledge
711 Third Avenue, New York, NY 10017

Routledge is an imprint of the Taylor & Francis Group, an informa business.

British Library Cataloguing-in-Publication Data
A catalogue record for this book is available from the British Library.

Library of Congress Cataloging-in-Publication Data
Nesti, Mark, 1959–
Youth development in football : lessons from the world's best academies /
    Mark Nesti and Chris Sulley.
        pages cm
    Includes bibliographical references and index.
    1. Soccer players—Training of—Cross-cultural studies.   2. Soccer
players—Recruiting—Cross-cultural studies.   3. Soccer teams—Cross-
cultural studies.   I. Sulley, Chris.   II. Title.
    GV943.9.T7N47 2015
    796.334—dc23
    2014022759

ISBN: 978-0-415-81498-0 (hbk)
ISBN: 978-0-415-81499-7 (pbk)
ISBN: 978-0-203-06650-8 (ebk)

Typeset in Bembo
by Apex CoVantage, LLC

For Arthur Piggott RIP – he loved his football

CONTENTS

ACKNOWLEDGEMENTS

It is usual practice to express gratitude to the publishing team at the end of an acknowledgements section. I would like to break with this tradition because it is no exaggeration to say that without the persistent and patient support shown by Simon Whitmore and Joshua Wells at Routledge, this project would have been an impossible undertaking. Knowing that Joshua and Simon have been so positive throughout all of the work, even during the delays brought on by job changes and unforeseen challenges, has been of such importance to both Chris and me.

I would also like to thank a number of other people who have helped me to bring this book to fruition. Direct support has come from my colleagues at Liverpool John Moores University, Drs Dave Richardson, Martin Littlewood and Martin Eubank, especially in regard to developing my thinking around the important concepts of identity and culture. As the most experienced University academic in the UK who has worked at youth levels in elite level professional football, Martin Littlewood has had the greatest influence on my thinking around player development in football. He has been generous in sharing his real-world knowledge and theoretical understanding derived from the years he has spent delivering sport psychology support inside several English Premier League clubs. I am also indebted to the many coaches and other back room staff I have worked alongside at first team and youth levels. I learned much from my involvement at Bolton Wanderers (2001–7), Newcastle United (2008–9) and Hull City (2008–10), and through work at other EPL clubs over the past 15 years. Most staff were genuinely passionate about their work with young players and spoke frequently about many of the topics covered in this book. I thank them for the education they provided, even when I did not always agree with their views or proposed solutions. In terms of my theoretical development and appreciation of the role of good coaching, I would like to mention Malcolm Cook; his insights based on work at all levels of the game have been a source of mental stimulation. I would also like to thank a small group of people I have encountered at various academic institutions throughout Europe and the world in the last 25 years who have encouraged me to locate my work within an existential psychology, phenomenology and person-centred perspective. They know who they are. Their courageous capacity to see psychology, development and learning as things that should not be cut adrift from values, morality, culture and philosophy has inspired me. This served to keep me motivated and ready to do battle, particularly when my views have been under threat from positivists and philosophical materialists on one side, or postmodernists on the other!

And finally, my co-author, Chris Sulley, has been key to providing some critical insight into the workings of the modern football Academy. He has listened patiently to my ideas over the years and corrected me when necessary, especially when I let theory become too important.

Mark Nesti

I have been very fortunate to have lived inside the professional football world most of my working life and on my journey have worked with some outstanding people that have influenced my thinking and shaped my philosophy as a coach and youth developer. Trying to list all these would be dangerous, as I feel I am bound to miss someone, but you know who you are and thank you for being part of my school of life.

A very sincere thanks goes to Simon Whitmore and Joshua Wells for their patience and guidance.

In regards to the development of this book, a very big thank you must go to Dr Mark Nesti, who has stimulated my thinking and used all of his experience to prod and push me into getting this book finished. I would also like to thank all those who were gracious enough to give me their time and insights into their club youth development programmes, especially Stanley Brard at Feyenoord.

A special dedication to Chris Dowling – grateful thanks for your help with proofreading and indexing.

Chris Sulley

1

INTRODUCTION

A number of developments have occurred during the past decade or so that have resulted in a great deal of interest in the health of youth football. It seems that almost everyone at some time or other has had something to say on the matter. Politicians, media commentators, academics and educators have joined those in the game itself to offer advice and identify what needs to be done. At an international level, FIFA, UEFA, ECA and most national governing bodies of football have carried out research, funded studies or employed consultants to help bring focus to their work with young players at amateur and professional levels of the sport.

Despite this, or maybe more worryingly, partly as a result of these efforts, the area appears to be full of contradictory views, competing diagnoses and radically different prognoses. The only thing it seems that all agree on is that there is a crisis and the status quo is no longer an option! Maybe one of the difficulties faced by football is that it can be very hard to separate mere assertion and speculation from genuinely evidence-based information. The cacophony of noise, whilst full of the best intentions, has arguably led to an impasse. Of more concern, it often appears that very little of real substance has changed, and in some places one gets the feeling that it is business as usual. However, this is not sustainable, not least because the future of the game literally depends on change and the young.

We hope that this book does not contribute more confusion and unhelpful suggestions by providing material that does not relate to the reality of developing youth footballers. Conversely, we hope that we have not been guilty of merely describing what is already well understood. Our overarching aim is to provide a critical account of what we have seen and experienced over many years' involvement in the professional game so that some clear recommendations can be made on the way forward. This work is not based on a set number of research studies, and neither is it derived solely from reflections on our applied experiences. What we have presented represents a synthesis of research findings, as well as ideas that have emerged from our practical engagement and professional roles we have occupied. We also believe that it is important to draw on theory and academic concepts to support our analysis to enable us to examine contentious proposals and positions that have been advocated and established by others in this area.

However, this is not meant to be the final word on youth development in professional football, and neither is this an attempt to address the topic from every possible academic discipline. To do this would require us to sacrifice depth for breadth. Therefore, we have decided to restrict ourselves to a social science perspective since this allows us to interrogate the story of youth development from an individual, organisational and cultural perspective. It is our belief that the insights offered by management theory, coaching studies, psychology, socio-psychology and, to some extent, cultural studies are most useful in assisting us to better understand the challenges we are currently facing.

Our hope is that we can offer a convincing argument that there are particular qualities and activities that represent best practice, and that these should become aspirations and eventually a reality for all in the near future. The exact and precise mechanisms to achieve this will depend upon the availability of resources and local and national conditions. Beyond this level of variation we will suggest that there are universal factors that must be attended to and put in place to increase the likelihood of achievement. One of these is that clubs must have a vision that drives their work in the area of youth development, and this must be owned and constantly renewed by the key stakeholders. The vision should be used to guide the club to produce players who can meet the demands of how the club wishes its first team players to play. This must not remain as a loose and merely philosophical aspiration; it must be articulated clearly in terms of what the club expects in relation to mentality, technical requirements, tactical acumen and physical parameters.

Tradition is another important word. The clubs we have encountered which contain many elements of best practice often have strong traditions. These could be more accurately described as living traditions, in that they are constantly being renewed to ensure they meet the present conditions. This type of tradition is something that serves a very specific purpose and is not merely about 'how things have always been done.' Rather, this is seen where clubs do not ignore their past, but strive continuously to bring it alive by embracing new ideas and behaviours that help them to drive towards their vision. Such traditions are not defensive, rigid or brittle and used to defend against needed change and innovation. They are malleable and dynamic and allow individuals and organisations to welcome new ideas and practices that build on the proven successes of a tradition. A living tradition helps clubs to avoid remaining in the past, relying on former achievements and trying (usually unsuccessfully) to reproduce these in very changed circumstances (Magee, 2002). A tradition that is a synthesis between the old and the new also lessens the temptation to constantly change things in order to be up to date and modern. This is sometimes even carried out at the expense of tried and tested philosophies and practices. The responsibility for maintaining the traditions that effect youth development at the club rests with everyone involved, although the senior staff will have the most important and influential role in this task (Gilson et al., 2001). The best clubs ensure that their traditions impact on everyone and everything; they also expect their leaders to defend and nurture their traditions in good times and bad!

The big issues

A number of very important themes are woven throughout the book. These are the importance of education, coaching, sport science and medicine, playing time and facilities. Education refers to football-specific, academic and general. It is for players, staff, coaches and parents. The best clubs place a great deal of attention on this aspect of their work. All agree that it is vital to delivering their goals of more and better equipped young players. Each club has taken a serious approach to this part of their duties, as can be seen from the planning, resources and energy that are committed to its success. A further striking commonality is that they seem to recognise that education is a long-term process. Their aim is to engender authentic learning, the type of learning that is permanent. This is because the learned content has become part of a person. This is in contrast to short-term information acquisition, something that is often paraded as true learning, but which usually fails when it's needed in practice.

Coaching is obviously one of the fundamental tasks that needs to be carried out. The best practice we have seen ensures that the coaching is guided by a thought-through philosophy that links closely to the everyday practice of all staff. Whilst the detail of what is coached and how this is conveyed to the players may vary considerably, there tends to be a common approach to the general role of the coach as the young players progress towards the first team professional environment. The usual pattern we see is that coaching moves from a more player-centred and less authoritarian style to a more directive and didactic approach as the players get older. However, in the best practice clubs this is not the general pattern. First, it seems that their philosophy is always player centred in that everything is done with their needs in mind, and not those of the coach or the system. Second, the coaching style becomes less, not more, didactic as the player develops; however, this does not mean that things become easier for the player! In fact, the reverse is true because the coaches tend to allow the players to find the solutions to the tactical, technical, physical or mental challenges they place in front of them. Feedback and focused advice are offered, but the expectation is that the players will become, in effect, their own coaches as they move through the ranks. It is also noticeable that the coaching is oriented towards placing the players in ever more stressful and potentially anxiety-inducing situations. This reveals that being player centred does not mean that players have an easy time, or that they are not placed in difficult circumstances.

The other very important issue relating to coaching is around the attitude towards practice time and how much of this amounts to deliberate practice (Ford and Williams, 2011). In our experience, most clubs fall far short of the 10,000 hours rule (Ericsson, 1993), and much of the work done could not be termed deliberate practice. In fact, some of the very best clubs in the world for youth development that we have visited and studied spend a sizeable part of their time on free play and small-sided games. Much of this appears to be an attempt to replicate the football that was played by children in an earlier period, whether on the streets, in the back-yard or on any piece of spare land. This was usually a highly competitive and skilful mini form of the game carried out without the guidance of adults or coaches. Such environments were ideally suited to the development of close control, touch, physi-cal resilience and decision making in tight spaces – some of the most essential skills and traits that we would expect to see in the elite level professional player.

Sport science and medical services are now an integral part of player care at most top-level professional football clubs. Provision of comprehensive support services has been extended to Academies and youth sections during the past 10–15 years. How-ever, how this is integrated into the coaching practice and education and indeed all functions in the youth sections in clubs are very varied. Some Academies and youth sections have attempted to model their sport science and medicine support on the systems and practices that operate at senior first team levels. Others tend to offer a less well-resourced and reduced version of the first team model. Some clubs do not appear to have a clear idea of what is the best version to meet their needs. We will attempt to identify what should be provided and how this can be best put to use.

In terms of the provision of facilities for youth development, the overwhelming majority of the best clubs have shared sites where first team and young players and their support staff are based together (Littlewood, 2005). At some this has been a deliberately planned option and is consistent with the vision of the club. For others the sharing of the same site has evolved rather than being the result of a carefully thought-out strategy. Irrespective of how the facilities have been designed, there is recognition by the best clubs of the very many benefits that emerge from having youth and senior players in the same place. For example, staff were keen to point out that the positives flow both ways. Young players get a first-hand experience of what is required to be a professional player, and the first team players are reminded about their important responsibilities as role models and guides to young players, some of whom will be the future of the club. In addition, clubs were aware that being on one site facilitated greater sharing of staff expertise between youth and first team staff, and that this helped to maintain open and constructive levels of communica-tion between each group. We will detail the benefits that occur as a result of this greater level of cooperation and understanding between the staff involved with young player development and those working at first team levels.

It's all in the mind

We believe that much of what takes place at clubs with a world-class reputation for youth development comes down to their mind-set. By this we do not mean that staff and players possess unique psychological skills that set them apart from others in the sport, but that there is strong evidence that the club's leaders continuously think about what they are trying to achieve (Gilson et al., 2001) and, crucially, are prepared to make brave decisions to try something new and even more challenging, or to return to practices and ideas that were successful in the past! The renewal of former excellence is sometimes a much harder task than coming up with novel suggestions because it requires humility and subtlety. That is, being sufficiently humble to realise you have made a mistake and to correct it; this is only possible by reintroducing something that has been discarded. The other aspect is that it is rarely possible or desirable to merely attempt to reproduce the past exactly since the changed conditions of the present make this impossible. What is often needed is to deliver the best from what was carried out before, but in a way that can meet modern circumstances. Not to do this is ultimately to provide something that, even if it is clearly needed and wanted, cannot be delivered in practice. The task is to be able to offer the substance of past good practices, but in a style that meets the current situation. This is not easy to achieve, especially if this is about a fundamental change. And in practice, it is impossible to deliver without thinking very carefully about why something must be done and how it can be actioned on the ground.

In our experience, the best clubs spend a great deal of time thinking about what they are doing and reflecting on different ways to achieve their goals. Even if no immediate or direct change in policy or practice emanates from this mental effort, there is a strong commitment to this way of behaving. These clubs expect this from individuals, from staff teams and from the organisation itself. This is seen in a number of tangible ways. Recruitment strategies are geared towards appointing people who possess a critical mind – those who are prepared to constantly challenge accepted views to ensure that only the best ideas and practices are embedded in the club and their work. Departmental teams are just that – not groups of individuals with specific qualifications and expertise but people who have the technical skills and knowledge for the job and are aware that those skills and knowledge are really effective only when they can be shared with other colleagues. Being able to work in a multidisciplinary and interdisciplinary environment is one of the greatest challenges Academy staff must confront, especially coaches, as it will be their responsibility to coordinate this and to some extent project manage to help the club fulfil its vision. Again this requires a particular type of individual and organisational psychology. At the individual level it needs individual staff who are prepared to share their knowledge with others because they are truly aware that this input is only a small part of the overall picture. This means that the club must appoint the very best qualified staff – those who know their area so thoroughly that they know what they don't know! These individuals must also have the moral character necessary that allows them to offer ideas that others may reject and be able to accept that their knowledge and skills have limitations. Having recruited such individuals, the organisation must be in a position to make best use of this group of outstanding practitioners. The best clubs ensure that they provide an organisational climate that will optimise their staff resource. In practice this means that these are usually highly organised, structured and focused environments. Although staff will usually not have formal and written job descriptions, they understand the organisational structures and operate within clear, dynamic and flexible systems. There are likely to be frequent meetings of both a planned and formal as well as a more *ad hoc* and informal variety. However, these factors in themselves would not be sufficient to guarantee that the clubs are able to make best use of the high-quality staff they have taken on. In addition to excellent organisational systems and procedures, the very best clubs possess a particular type of culture. Very different to areas like resources and finance, the type of culture a club creates is essentially something under its own control. We will examine this in several of the chapters since, according to the work of Wilson (2001), this factor is ultimately the most important in how close the club comes to achieving its vision, aims and goals.

And finally, from a more traditional psychological perspective, we consider the role of sport psychology in youth development and identify best practice. This area is given special attention because we believe that it is one of the least understood and most poorly applied aspects of practice in professional football in general, and with young players in particular. Despite considerable attempts to increase awareness and knowledge about this area in many countries, it continues to be the most under-used part of sport science support in football. In discussing some of the reasons behind this, we hope to highlight why clubs remain unsure about the value of sport psychology support and identify what they are looking for from the sport psychology profession. It is quite surprising that so few clubs have a carefully planned and systematic approach to the provision of sport psychology support, despite all without exception identifying that the psychological make-up of the player is ultimately the most important predictor of success with youth footballers.

Finally, there are some broader psychological factors that are clearly identifiable at the best clubs. We will address these by considering how theory and research in sport psychology point towards the importance of encouraging particular types of motivation in young athletes, and how footballing skills are most easily and effectively acquired. There is a vast amount of research on skill acquisition, although most of it is not based on studies in professional and elite level football.

The clubs and their staff are aware that in some cases, young people's passion and love for the game is being overtaken by some very powerful and influential competing attractions. Changes in society, from transport to employment patterns, and from family structure to the role of parents, have had a major impact on the way in which clubs are constrained in their work with young players. It does seem that whilst many clubs are aware of these major changes, there has not been an adequate response to them, although the new Elite Player Performance Plan (EPPP) in England Category 1 and 2 clubs will have to provide this support for the players. Again it is about being able to have an impact on those factors that are more in control of the clubs and increasing awareness about those matters that are societally based.

The debate about practice regimes, and the duration of practice and methods, has been around for at least the past two decades. Some clubs have evolved their own answers to these questions. In contrast, others seem to be unsure and are awaiting a lead from governing bodies and other experts. However, one of the consistent themes across best practice clubs is that they try to maintain a play philosophy that could inform practice at all age groups and not just for the very youngest. How this was achieved tended to vary quite differently between clubs, but all were united in their belief that serious play was the best way to develop players for the future. The word *play* is rarely discussed or subjected to an in-depth analysis, possibly because it is assumed that everyone knows its meaning. However, a review of the way this term is used to cover so many different activities, and that academic disciplines offer such very different definitions, points towards the importance of understanding what this word precisely refers to. This is considered in this book by looking at the psychology of play, flow and intrinsic motivation; looking at what are the benefits in terms of learning and overall motivation; and discussing how this can be accommodated in work with young players.

Key words

Our engagement with the practice of youth development in high level professional football has led us to identify a number of important words and phrases that we have heard expressed time and again in the clubs. Some of these terms are borrowed from the worlds of research, academia and theory. Others are from the treasure trove of the game itself, from its traditions and the past, as well as from more recent times.

It is possible to view these words in relation to culture, organisational processes and demands placed on the individual. Although it is fair to say that most of the best practice clubs we have encountered have an overarching culture that extends from the first team to the youth section, it is possible to speak about this in relation to youth development in isolation.

The best cultures we have seen are those where there is a commitment to particular values governing the behaviour of all those working at the Academy. Values in turn impact on the ethics that underpin practice. These values are imbued with moral content; they point towards an agreed morality. Most usually this is something felt and sensed rather than written about and documented. The type of culture in an organisation can be seen in practice and permeates the whole environment. It is a kind of unseen hand that directs behaviour between individuals, within groups and across the club or Academy. However, this does not mean that it is not about very tangible and key issues. The culture represents the collective morality of an organisation; it provides the framework that proscribes and prohibits particular types of behaviour. In more straightforward terms, culture is the visible sign of who we really are beyond systems and processes. It is about what we stand for, and what we consider to be right and wrong.

It is striking that the more successful clubs in youth development are those with clear convictions about the type of culture they are trying to create and sustain. Staff, and to some extent the players themselves, should be able to identify what the culture is like and, most importantly, why it is that way. There may be specific staff who are able to articulate more fully the details that support the culture and describe the philosophy behind it. However, the more important issue is whether individuals know what they are required to do in the culture, and how this will assist them to fulfil their potential.

It is at this point that players, coaches and other support staff begin to talk about the need to operate in a culture where trust is viewed as essential. *Trust* means knowing that something can be relied upon, and that this will operate in difficult and good moments equally. Trust is closely connected with honesty and respect. Cultures where there is a high degree of trust are those where individuals can rely on others to carry out their jobs and tasks without deception, dishonesty or slander. This is what is really meant by adopting a person-centred approach in a particular club or environment.

Without trust, little can be achieved beyond the short term, and the best youth developers are focused on the long term as much as more immediate goals. A culture of trust engenders greater sharing of ideas between individuals and departments. Holistic approaches and interdisciplinary work are more possible since confidence to collaborate grows if people can see that the aim is for all to benefit rather than for some to strengthen their position at the expense of others. Without engendering a culture of trust, there will be little appetite for teamwork, transparency of communication and striving for a common goal. The best clubs ensure that trust is continually protected and strengthened to help individuals and groups to leave their defences behind and become a genuine community − one with a clear vision that supports a specific philosophy of practice that can be summed up in the well-known but rarely seen maxim of, 'all for one, and one for all!'

Although it may sound impractical and idealistic, developing and maintaining a culture of trust is vital to the success of the youth development section of a professional football club. The responsibility for this task lies with everyone connected with youth work at the club; however, there are some key individuals who arguably have a more important role to play in this. The evidence suggests that this group includes the club's owners, the manager, the Academy or youth development manager and the director of performance or sport psychologist. The best clubs are those where these individuals in particular act to shape the culture and help it to evolve towards a healthy state where actions are evaluated against their effect on the common good. In order to achieve this in practice, though, there must be a commitment to some other key terms.

Our engagement and research in this area has revealed that three words are of great importance in creating this kind of culture: subsidiarity, autonomy and responsibility. The first of these refers to the capacity to devolve decision making to the lowest levels. This means that, where possible, decision-making powers should be passed down to those closest to the action. This is because of a belief that the best decisions are likely to be made by those with the most comprehensive and detailed knowledge of the situation. It is also based on the sound idea that those closest to the work are most sensitive to the impact of their decisions and possess greater understanding of the context. This means that their decisions will be easier to explain and will be based on both hard and softer data that sometimes is unavailable to those higher up.

Closely related to this is the notion of autonomy. This means allowing individuals and groups the opportunity to formulate their own decisions and put these into practice. This is a way to empower staff and help develop motivation and confidence. It is also the optimum approach to ensuring that an organisation demonstrates that it trusts the people it has employed and is prepared to accept that they have the skills to carry out their roles.

Finally, there is the important concept of responsibility. Autonomy without responsibility is licence rather than freedom. Left unchecked it will lead to chaos and anarchy and a breakdown in the culture of trust. The best practices we have witnessed are where staff are comfortable with the idea that they will be held accountable for their decisions and the work they undertake. They do not view this as a threat to their freedom to carry out their jobs, but see it as a sign that the club is concerned about employing individuals who care personally about what they do. Those who are merely doing a job, or carrying out some work they care little about, are less likely to see responsibility for their actions as a positive because they are using these activities for their own ends. In contrast, individuals who approach their work as more of a vocation, that is, something they are committed to personally and professionally, will likely welcome responsibility and scrutiny of their activities.

These types of cultures are usually prepared to adopt a scientific and rational perspective to assist their work. This means that there will be attention to detail, careful use of measurement and integration of science to enhance performance in areas like psychology, physical fitness and match analysis. It is common to hear the view expressed that a scientific culture is one where there is an overreliance on formal methods, systems and planning at the expense of intuition, personal communication and flexibility. This dualistic thinking is prevalent in academic thinking and in our culture as a whole. However, within the best Academies there is a different atmosphere. In these types of cultures it is not about whether science or practice-based knowledge is most valued. Instead, focus is directed at how improvements can be best achieved. Sometimes this is led by scientific knowledge, and at other times decisions may be based more on applied practice and past experience. Often it is derived from a synthesis of what the best science indicates and what craft knowledge suggests. For this to happen constructively, there needs to be a culture that is open to new ideas irrespective of where these come from. This will allow the organisation and individual staff to interpret the data and the information available, and convert it to useable knowledge that can inform genuine learning. The best clubs in the world nurture this type of culture to make sure that the club does not allow itself to narrowly and exclusively follow either the new approaches and science or the past and tradition.

At an organisational level, we would expect to see certain things in place that are often absent in clubs that are less effective in youth development – for example, regular meetings to keep communication lines open and action staff to move things forward; access to a greater pool of expertise; and joined-up thinking in the critical areas of recruitment, player support and coaching practice.

These elite clubs have transparent and logical organisational structures. Staff know their job responsibilities, and management and leadership roles are well understood and support the organisational aims. Recruitment policies are adhered to and are devised to ensure that the best qualified staff are attracted and retained. Little is left to chance. Best practice at youth development means that best practice is evident in terms of the organisational processes; these are continually reviewed to ensure they are effective and efficient (Brady et al., 2008).

Other important concerns can be viewed from a more individual perspective. The top Academies ensure that players have the opportunity to engage in competition, leagues and matches to acquire game understanding and practice their skills in challenging situations. They also attempt to instil a culture of play. This informs all that they do and is part of the underlying performance philosophy. Play here does not mean non-serious, easy or comfortable activity. Neither is it seen as being about uncommitted behaviour or lacking in drive and motivation. Instead, this key word, *play*, was used to explain the importance of small-sided games, individual learning, intrinsic motivation and creativity. A psychology of play could clearly be detected through the practice and theory governing young players' development in the sport. This was being used to help players acquire greater levels of resilience, inventiveness, courage, spontaneity and spirit.

Other important terms often mentioned at the most successful clubs were those of stress, anxiety (Jones, 1995), confidence, self-esteem, mental toughness (Crust, 2007) and identity. These were addressed in a variety of ways. Sometimes this was carried out with the support of sport psychologists, but more often this was delivered through the work of other support staff and coaches. In this area of the clubs' activities, there was recognition that families had a major positive role to play. Parents and families were seen as one of the most important factors to assist the club in producing outstanding young footballers who could progress to professional levels. Again, what is very noticeable was that the best clubs fully involved the parents in their task, but they did this in a focused, consistent and methodical way. All were viewed as important to the aims of the club. More important, all parents were treated, and seen to be treated, as equally important no matter how well their son performed.

Chapter content

This book is divided into eight chapters, each addressing important topics that clubs must attend to if they hope to provide the best environment for youth development. The chapter headings reflect the way in which the clubs we have visited and worked with have structured their activities. They are also informed by the recommendations of various football governing bodies across the world. Finally, we have tried to link these where possible to the guidance from the EPPP (The Premier League, 2011) that was launched by the English Premier League (EPL) and the Football League (FL) on 1 July 2012.

The first part of the text concentrates on matters relating to strategy, structures and organisational concerns. These are areas that the best clubs address fully, but importantly, in ways that connect to their philosophy, values and traditions. Their approach suggests strongly that compliance with external regulations and ensuring that sound organisational processes are in place does not mean that all clubs must do the same thing. They have found methods and practices that enable them to conform without becoming something they are uncomfortable with. As we will discuss, this has been adopted as a deliberate strategy by the clubs and is often something that has evolved over time. Unlike some of the research evidence we will examine relating to approaches at many other clubs, the best practice clubs often do more than what is required of them to meet the regulations. Indeed, it could be argued that many of the guidelines for youth development emanating from various bodies across the world owe as much to what these clubs have done for many years as to genuinely new thinking or radical ideas.

Chapter 2 considers how the game as a whole and the football industry attempt to provide direction to help clubs achieve their aims in the area of youth development. Governance is concerned with matters of finance, legal regulations, rules and satisfying football governing body stipulations. These must be satisfactorily adhered to. They will directly impact on how the club conducts its business externally and how it organises its activities internally. Governance is primarily about ensuring that the club operates in an ethically sound, financially robust and legally correct way. It is also about developing operational codes of practice and systems that will allow the club to finance its activity in a responsible and sustainable fashion.

We will also reflect on the impact of various directives from FIFA, UEFA, the English Premier League and the FA, as these attempt to help shape youth development in professional football in the years ahead.

In Chapter 2 we also consider the topic of vision and strategy. The best clubs have clearly articulated strategies, and these are usually derived from an agreed-upon vision of what they are aiming to achieve. There has been some research which suggests that many clubs have utilised an *ad hoc* approach rather than following a deliberate and carefully formulated strategy in the area of youth development. We will critically analyse some of this evidence and identify how and why the approach adopted in the best clubs is different to this.

Having a vision that can help guide the club through difficult situations and rapidly changing environments is something that was evident in the majority of best practice clubs. We will consider how their particular vision for youth development was identified, and how this affects activities in practice at ground level.

Good leadership and skilful management are vital elements in any organisation. The best clubs take great care to appoint staff with the requisite knowledge, skills and experience to manage their programmes and provide inspirational leadership. At some clubs this is achieved through quite a formal and structured approach, whereas at others there is a looser methodology. However, in each there is considerable attention paid to making sure that the person appointed to the post has both the technical skill and qualifications needed, as well as the personal qualities necessary to succeed in what can be a very fast moving and pressurised environment. For some clubs this means that they tend to recruit from within so that they can be confident in knowing how the person will react in demanding situations. This is also seen as a way to remove doubts about the issues of loyalty, and their motivation in the job and future aspirations.

Leadership and management are not just about specific people and roles, or structures and procedures. The best clubs attempt to include all staff in the management processes through formal and informal mechanisms. For example, these include the use of appraisal and staff development systems and, at a more informal level, creating a climate where staff are encouraged to provide feedback and communicate openly and freely. The literature suggests that this is something many clubs are unable to do well, and that there is often a lack of commitment to this because it is seen as a threat to group cohesion and team harmony. In contrast, the best clubs tend to reject this view and have established leadership styles and management cultures that are designed to encourage greater shared involvement in decision making and activity across all levels and roles. We will describe in Chapter 3 how this approach impacts on youth development processes at the best clubs, and why they are so strongly committed to working in this way.

The second section of the book looks at some of the more traditional topics associated with youth development in football. These are more focused on the players and the experience they will encounter at the club.

Chapter 4 is concerned with talent identification and recruitment. There has been extensive research in this area over the past 20 years dealing with a wide range of issues. For example, some studies have investigated the technical, physical and motor skill parameters associated with the concept of footballing talent. Other work has looked more closely at the issue of talent itself and analysed differing accounts of this idea and what this could mean for those involved in talent identification in youth football. From a more socio-psychological and sports development perspective, work has been carried out on talent identification and recruitment systems and recommendations offered about the most effective approaches. We will critically evaluate a selection of this empirical work and discuss how it relates to what we have seen at some of the best clubs in youth development in football.

In conclusion, we have found that this topic is one of the most debated in the sport; the future of the game depends on how well this is addressed. In this chapter it is very evident that the best clubs are guided by both the scientific research and by their own previous practice. In order to be able to use both of these sources of information in a way that helps the clubs achieve their aims, there must be a number of important factors in place. We will review these and provide examples of how the best clubs manage this. This will begin to reveal how their approach to scientific research allows them to extract the most useful information from this and convert it into useable knowledge to guide practice.

Once players are recruited, the club must provide education and welfare support. There are many different approaches to the provision of education for young players in clubs; however, the best are acutely aware of how important this area of work is. They tend to view this as being a cornerstone to helping the players to become better footballers through becoming accomplished learners. Time and again we have seen that whilst many clubs view education as a distraction from the main task of becoming a professional footballer, the best clubs are genuinely convinced that being well educated is a positive and is helpful in supporting the overall development of players. A closer examination of this philosophy reveals that these clubs acknowledge that their task is to produce rounded individuals who will be capable of understanding the game and themselves more fully as they develop.

In a similar way, the enlightened clubs have excellent support in place to provide for players' welfare. Again, they know that young footballers will learn and improve more easily and quickly in a culture where they are cared for, rather than one where they are left to fend for themselves. The research carried out over many years indicates that this area of a club's responsibilities has not always been met adequately. Sometimes this may be because of finance or lack of resources, or due to a failure to take this work seriously. Of greater concern, some of the literature suggests that clubs do not see the value in this type of support and may even view it as undermining the motivation, resilience and mental toughness (Cook et al., 2014) they try to engender into the players. We will look at these issues in Chapter 3.

Chapters 4, 5, 6 and 7 are directly concerned with how the young player should benefit from the expertise at the club in terms of coaching, sport science and sport psychology. The first of these areas has been subject to the greatest amount of research interest in the sport as a whole. The value of different coaching styles, how best to impart knowledge and how to educate and train coaches are some of the key topics that have been addressed. We will look carefully at how the philosophies and practices in coaching and coach education in the best clubs compare with the findings from the published scientific research. There is little doubt that high-quality coaching can improve learning and development, and there are some common views on how this can be achieved.

At other times it sometimes seems that clubs have been guilty of failing to adapt the coaching models and philosophies that have the strongest support from the scientific literature. It does appear that they often prefer to continue to use their own way of working and try to ignore alternatives that they are unfamiliar with. Less common, but equally damaging, some clubs tend to uncritically follow the latest ideas on coaching or sport science, often without any in-depth understanding of what they are doing.

We note in several chapters that the best clubs are very aware of their preferred coaching philosophy and style, and how sport science should be used to enhance player performance. Paradoxically, this involves them adopting a continually questioning approach to their own methods and to the recommendations from the research literature and other sources. In sport science in particular, we have seen that the best clubs devote as much time to scrutinising and eventually rejecting new ideas as they do to implementing changes guided by the scientific research. It is interesting to observe that how much sport science features in the practice of coaches can vary significantly. Despite such variation, the underlying understanding about the value of this area and how it can be integrated to improve performance is remarkably similar across the best clubs in youth development.

The final chapter contains a series of recommendations that we feel are the most important for youth development in professional football. This is not meant to close down future debate about the best way forward by providing an exhaustive list. Rather, it represents what we have seen, heard and been involved with at some of the most effective youth development football clubs in the professional game worldwide.

Methodology

The ideas presented and discussed in this book have emerged from a number of different sources. These include the professional experiences of the two authors, academic research and material gathered as part of a year long funded study into best practice in elite football Academies. This was carried out by the second author throughout one season. In this chapter, we will outline how this research was conducted and look at the way in which the data that emerged has been used in the book.

We also feel that it is important to include brief yet detailed autobiographical accounts specifically focusing on our experiences in professional football. These personal histories not only helped shape our thinking in relation to research analysis but also, of equal importance, provided us with data from the lived world of applied practice. In compiling this book, we have drawn extensively on our work in youth and senior level professional football, particularly in the areas of management, coaching, sport psychology and sport science. We are convinced that the craft knowledge acquired through working alongside so many dedicated and highly skilled staff in professional football should be shared with others. That this data has not emerged from a formal research study is not a weakness in our view. We believe that it has allowed us to test research and theory against practice, and ensure that findings from our own study at the clubs across Europe were subject to a thorough critical analysis. The result, we hope, is that the material presented provides a bridge between two ways of creating knowledge – the type based on systematic and rigorous research, and that derived from real world practice. Unfortunately, it is quite rare to see this type of hybrid approach in the literature. For example, books about football are usually grounded in theory and scientific research, or they ignore this and present an atheoretical and practical perspective. Although these can serve a very useful function, they are by definition one-sided. More worryingly, they can inadvertently give the impression that their view should dominate future work and developments. And at their worst, the weaknesses of each approach can leave the student of the game frustrated. Theory-based literature incorporating the latest research studies can seem impractical and lacking context. Conversely, practice-based accounts can appear simplistic and shallow.

We acknowledge that in trying to overcome this tension there is the risk that what is produced is neither good scientific work nor a sound account of practice. However, despite these difficulties and challenges, we feel that methodological purity should sometimes be sacrificed to allow new ideas to be presented. To the rigorous scientist this will be a step too far. For the non-scientist there may well be concern that generalisations and broad claims are offered when experienced practitioners know that these concepts are rarely if ever found on the ground. This should make the book an equally uncomfortable read for both the more scientifically minded individual and the practitioner. If this is the case, then we have succeeded in one of our aims at least, which is to contribute in a small but significant way to encouraging a greater synthesis between different forms of acquiring and disseminating knowledge and understanding in relation to best practices in youth development in football.

Research methods

Background

The aim of the research was to identify best practice at some of the most successful football clubs in the world for youth development. The second author was appointed to carry out funded research for an English Premier League club so they could draw lessons from well-established and highly regarded youth football Academies in Europe. The project timescale was one year from collection of data to dissemination of the final report. With the agreement of the club, the first author was given permission to use their research findings to write this book to enable a wider audience to benefit from the work that was carried out.

Participating clubs and organisations

Visits were made to the following clubs (7) and football organisations (3): Bayer Leverkusen, Barcelona, Feyenoord, Ajax, AJ Auxerre, Bayern Munich, Middlesbrough, KNVB, FFF (Clairefontaine) and Aspire (Qatar).

These were chosen due to the outstanding reputation they had for youth development and/or because of the resources they had devoted to this part of the game over a number of years. The second author also had excellent working relationships with some of the key individuals in youth football at each of these locations; this ensured that a mixed methods approach to data collection could be utilised more effectively.

Data collection

Initial contact was made with the Academy director or other senior staff member who had responsibility for the coordination of youth player development. Each club or national governing body was visited for an average time period of 10 days. The research aims were explained to all staff prior to data collection.

Formal interviews that were audio recorded were carried out with up to 10 staff members at each venue. This data was supplemented by informal conversations, observation of practices, attendance at meetings and socialising with key staff outside the training ground. In essence, the visits at each club resembled a type of mini ethnographic study; the researcher was able to immerse himself in the day-to-day activities of the organisation and gain a perspective from the vantage point of a trusted and knowledgeable insider to some extent. The previous experience of the researcher as an Academy Director, high level coach and former professional player (see autobiography below) assisted the data collection process in a number of ways.

First, it helped the staff to feel quickly at ease and open up to someone they could recognise as having shared experiences of their professional world. Second, this personal and professional background helped the researcher to guide the informal dialogue they engaged in and the observations they made towards the key issues and important concerns. Third, it allowed the researcher to build a level of trust with key staff so they would feel more prepared to speak freely about their views, even and especially where these differed from the official policies of their professional bodies, other colleagues or employers.

Data trustworthiness

The personal and lengthy engagement at each club and organisation allowed the researcher to meet the same individuals several times throughout the visit. This provided an opportunity to ask further questions based on what had been observed or picked up in earlier conversations, and to revisit interview data to ensure that this was as accurate and comprehensive as possible. In this way data trustworthiness was enhanced.

Data analysis

All interview data was transcribed verbatim. This was then subject to a thorough thematic analysis. Theme headings were partly informed by academic literature and more recent terminology based on the EPPP documentation, as well as reports from football governing bodies at national and supranational levels.

We then added data from our own applied experiences to the research findings. Whilst we acknowledge that this procedure would be unacceptable in a traditional scientific study, we feel that it allowed us to add something important to the work overall. We drew constantly on our different experiences, qualifications and knowledge in deciding what to report and how this should be presented and, finally, discussed and analysed. The aim was not to report all of the themes we uncovered; rather, we hoped to highlight what we considered to be the most important. This might be because they offered new accounts of familiar topics, or provided unexpected support for previous research or ideas about youth development in football.

To conclude, this work is not meant to be a comprehensive account of the findings from a carefully designed longitudinal scientific research project. Instead, the intention was to draw on data and information from a variety of sources to generate some new insights into youth development based on what the authors have acquired through their study, research and applied activities in professional football.

Football autobiographies

Chris Sulley

Chris has spent most of his life immersed in professional football and, in particular, youth development. His football talent was developed on the streets and on the playgrounds during the 1960s and was soon recognised when he was selected for South London boys under 12. This was followed by an invitation to join Chelsea Football Club for special tuition, as young players were not allowed to sign any forms until the age of 14, known as the Associated Schoolboy Forms. Officially, boys were not supposed to train more than one hour per week with a professional football club until they were 14 years old. Fortunately, they were able to train twice per week and during holidays played games wearing the Chelsea kit.

Having been invited to join Chelsea at the age of 12, he subsequently signed apprenticeship forms and later professional forms, so he has the experience and knowledge of what it takes to be a professional footballer. In 1981 his playing career took him to Bournemouth, where they won promotion in his first season, won the first Associated Members Cup and beat Manchester United in the third round of the FA Cup. Having spent five years at Bournemouth, he was transferred to Dundee United, where he played a minor role in their most memorable achievement – getting to the UEFA Cup final in 1987. Unfortunately, he was unable to gain regular first team football and quickly moved on to Blackburn Rovers, where he won the Full Members Cup and eventually, after their fourth attempt, gained promotion via the playoffs to the top league in 1992. He then played one season at Port Vale and two seasons at Preston North End before being invited onto John Beck's coaching staff, where he took up the position of Head of Youth, with specific duties for the Youth team. While there, he also revamped the whole youth development programme as a more professional era was emerging. During Chris's coaching spell at Preston, he worked with players such as Kevin Kilbane, Paul McKenna and David Lucas, with Andrew Lonergan emerging as a future talent. In 1996 he was invited to join Blackburn Rovers as their Assistant Head of Centre of Excellence, which included working across all the age groups from under 9 to under 19. He was very fortunate to work with a talented group of young players that included David Dunn, Damien Duff and Damien Johnson. In 1998 the Academy system was introduced under the banner of the 'Blueprint for Football' and, although the criteria were quite stringent, 38 clubs out of the 92 joined the scheme, with Bolton Wanderers being one of them. The experiences gained gave rise to an invitation by Bolton Wanderers for Chris to initially become their under 19's coach, but he very quickly became the Academy manager, where he grew the whole operation from four full-time staff to 18 full-time staff and an army of part-time staff to create one of the first multidisciplinary teams in the new Academy structures. Players such as Kevin Nolan, Joey O'Brien and Recardo Vaz Tê were some of the products of this development programme. The search for talent took him around the world to places such as France, Brazil, Australia and many more. He also spawned the creation of the International Academy, which gives the opportunity to young footballers around the world to taste the Bolton Wanderers' philosophy. He also developed the Coach Education department, which was another way of putting back something into the community, as well as providing opportunities for young coaches to be mentored and helping with talent identification of coaches and young players.

In 2008, Chris left Bolton Wanderers and spent time as a consultant for various professional football organisations and was able to use some of his vast experiences in more academic environments. Having gained his MBA in 2000, he was able to lecture at University of Central Lancashire, Liverpool John Moores University and Myerscough College whilst keeping a keen interest in the professional game. Chris also gained his FA Tutor status in the new youth awards and UEFA 'B' Licence. It was during this time in 2010 that Chris was approached to conduct a major piece of research that involved visiting some of the best professional football youth development programmes in the world and looking at their structures and operations over a 10-month period. This work mainly consisted of interviews with Academy Managers and other key staff. For example, Barcelona gave a full PowerPoint presentation outlining their whole youth development programme followed by observations of coaches working with their players, which confirmed that their philosophy was congruent with their coach behaviours. National centres like Aspire in Qatar allowed us to visit for a week and spend time with all the key staff involved in the development programme to get a feel of how this multidisciplinary environment operated.

Chris was appointed as Academy Manager at Leeds United in 2011 but due to a lack of support left to take up a role with the Football Association in 2012, which involved mentoring coaches to gain their mandatory coaching qualifications but also their onward professional development. The move towards mentoring Academy coaches has been one of the new initiatives that is really adding value to the new Academy environment, and Everton Football Club recognised this by inviting Chris to join them in 2013.

Mark Nesti

Mark was appointed in 2008 as an associate professor of psychology in sport at Liverpool John Moores University. He is a British Psychological Society Chartered sport psychologist with over 25 years' experience working in sports. Although he has been an academic and sport psychology consultant for most of this period, Mark was formerly a sports development manager and sports council officer. Despite his background in sport science and sport psychology, he has spent much of his time working alongside coaches, development officers, sports administrators and teachers. Through this he has gained an understanding of the importance of good governance and the value of adopting a strategic perspective to maximise sporting opportunity at grassroots and high level performance. He has been involved with youth sport projects throughout the years in a range of sports and has extensive experience doing applied work with elite level athletes and coaches. It is this area of sport on which most of his writing has concentrated until recently. However, as we shall see, he believes that much of what senior sports performers encounter is fundamentally little different than the challenges faced by younger participants.

In terms of his own practical involvement in football, Mark played county, semi-professional and University football. Introduced to the game in the late 1960s,

Mark grew up during an era in British football that was well before the advent of youth development centres and Academies. In the 1960s and '70s, talent identification tended to be very unsystematic, and many young players were overlooked or remained undiscovered, especially if they lived beyond the main urban areas. The popularity of the game in these years and the limited resources of the clubs combined to mean that there was little motivation driving the clubs and governing bodies to approach youth development and talent identification in a more rigorous and systematic way.

The dominant working-class traditions of the game in the UK also meant that young players from outside this socio-economic group often struggled for recognition. This was also a period when many in the clubs were reluctant to take on youngsters who were also academically capable. The fear seemed to be that when the demands of the game became too much, these young players would abandon the sport and return to the safer world of education. This experience of being unconsidered by the professional game whilst being told by coaches and peers that you had the ability to 'make it' contributed to a particular mind-set towards the game for Mark. In simple terms, although he remained passionate about football, Mark became very motivated to help ensure equity of opportunity so fewer players would be missed. He recognises that his own story is shared by many people, and over the years he has seen how important luck can be at the different stages of development for young players hoping to enter the professional game. And now, after extensive applied experience as a sport psychologist, Mark has come across players who in private acknowledge how fortunate they have been to get a chance in the game. Although aware of their own footballing ability, these players also mention the importance of having benefitted from good advice from parents, high-quality coaching, being brought up in the right area or other advantages that helped them achieve in the game. He has also worked alongside and supported many individuals who were unlucky enough to be rejected along the way; some of these players feel they were never given a fair chance to succeed and have left the game bitter and disillusioned. The reality of how close the margin is between success and failure remains today, just as it was in the past. This may seem to be a surprising claim, especially when clubs generally adopt a much more serious and well-resourced effort at identifying and developing young players. However, it should be remembered that despite new ways of capturing objective data and increasing investment in key processes, the decisions that must be made about players are still and *must be* infused with subjectivity. Deciding is a human enterprise; data and information can assist this action, but ultimately the individual person must decide without full and complete knowledge. This is unavoidable. And partly as a result of this, there will be occasions where good players will be missed or removed, and others with less ability and talent will progress and achieve.

Having lived some of this in his own encounter with the sport and spending over two decades working with professional football, Mark is aware of how important sound approaches to youth development are in the game at all levels. This awareness has been heightened by carrying out sport psychology work with first team professional footballers, many at English Premier League clubs. During 2001/2 to 2009/10, Mark worked inside three clubs delivering sport psychology support to players and staff at first team levels. Engagement ranged from 2–3 days a week at Bolton Wanderers to up to 5 days a week at Newcastle United and Hull City. Much of the work centred on providing confidential sport psychology counselling sessions to first team and development squad players. Typically, this took place at the clubs and involved upwards of 10 one-on-one scheduled meetings each week. From a theoretical perspective, much of what was discussed in these sessions was about identity, trying to remain authentic in a challenging environment and dealing with performance stress arising from organisational and individual sources (Nesti, 2010). One of the most important underlying themes to emerge was about the importance of maintaining a balanced approach. This involved the players reminding themselves that they needed to maintain the paradoxical psychological profile that Csikszentmihalyi (1996) reported from his research with over 100 CEOs of major companies, elite sport performers and academics. The profile that emerged described individuals who were strongly self-confident yet humble, firm and flexible, systematic and creative, shaped by deeply held values yet able to remain open to new ideas. In his applied work with high level professional players, Mark came across this paradoxical psychological profile in many of the most successful staff and players.

This applied experience in professional football linked closely to Mark's interest in existential phenomenological psychology (Nesti, 2004); this approach adopts a holistic perspective and argues that happiness and well-being come from striving to be fully oneself despite the difficulties this can bring. In applied terms, it means that players and staff were encouraged to embrace the anxiety associated with facing up to new choices and accept the responsibility for the decisions they make. This approach to psychology is opposed largely to the use of techniques to help individuals feel better through removal of symptoms (Corlett, 1996a). Instead, the focus is on embracing discomfort and anxiety as something that often accompanies growth, change and learning.

Surprisingly, or rather not when one thinks about it, the existential view seems to have something valuable to offer in terms of understanding the challenges of those who work at the youth levels in football. Although mental skills training in such things as pre-performance routines, goal setting and positive self-talk can be useful at an early stage of development, players will also find themselves in very demanding situations that cannot be addressed through application of these skills alone. For example, they will face a number of critical moments (Nesti and Littlewood, 2011) and transitions (Brown and Potrac, 2009) throughout their time in the Academy. These can include periods of prolonged deselection, communication issues with coaches and other staff, pressure from parents, match-related demands, educational expectations and failure to secure a contract. These are similar to some of the challenges facing professional players in the first team environment, albeit that the expectations around performance and results are far greater.

These applied experiences within the English Premier League have also impacted on Mark's views about coaching practice, coach education and sport science in football.

It has led him to question some of the theory and research that has come up in the past 20 or more years about football performance. This has particularly been the case with work that purports to be about elite level players at first team or youth levels. Much of the research and theorising seems to lack ecological validity in the area because it does not involve high level players and is often detached from real-world practice.

In terms of the impact from working alongside highly capable staff such as those at Bolton Wanderers during the Sam Allardyce and Mike Forde era (1999–2007), Mark has observed that the best often operate like practitioner-scientists. Unlike the currently fashionable term of scientist-practitioner, a practitioner-scientist views the context and demands of real-world application as the primary factor to consider; science is used creatively to guide rather than drive decisions and actions. The best staff who operate this way are always open to new ideas and the potential contributions of scientific thought and research. This helps them to avoid becoming stuck in the past and restricted by moribund traditions. Instead, they maintain the best of the old ways by continually renewing or rejecting these through exposure to different ideas and ways of working, especially those emanating from the social and natural sciences, coaching and management theory and research.

Holistic approaches

In conclusion, much of the material for this book has been strongly influenced by the unique individual and professional experiences that Chris and Mark have had in football. Mark's interest has been focused on the psychological dimension, whilst Chris has drawn more from his background in coaching and coach education. However, both have had leadership roles in the sport and have had to work closely with education and welfare staff, medical personnel and sports scientists. Although they have learned a considerable amount from all the clubs, staff and players with whom they have worked, the most important experience in terms of providing material for this book is based on the roles they occupied at Bolton Wanderers in the English Premier League. Bolton gained a well-deserved reputation during an eight-year spell, under the audacious and dynamic leadership of Sam Allardyce, for being one of the most advanced clubs in world football in terms of sport science provision. The first team and Academy back room staff contained several individuals with master's and doctoral level qualifications, and others with extensive experience at all levels of the game. The guiding principle at all times was that everything that was done should be aimed at enhancing player performance. Coaching, player support, sport science and any other forms of input and support could be justified only on this basis. In very simple terms, if something assisted the team in getting good results, it was welcomed; if it did not, it was removed. This philosophy was consistently applied to specific practices, interventions, equipment and staff. As a result of this, the club used a wide range of approaches, and the organisational climate was one where innovation, creativity and originality were expected. Staff were empowered to operate this way; there was considerable autonomy and support for independent decision making. On the other side, all staff were expected to accept responsibility for their actions and be able to maintain strong levels of intrinsic motivation towards their work, especially during the inevitable phases of poor performances and bad results. This culture of freedom and responsibility was underpinned by a very clear operational philosophy. There is a need to act quickly, decisively and correctly in such a fast-moving environment where a run of five or six consecutive games without a win can lead to a change in management and staff at first team levels, and great disruption in the Academy. Because of this, the best clubs will support their staff fully, but if work is not up to the desired levels, they are unafraid to change approach, abandon methods or sack staff. To ensure that this is carried out in a fair and appropriate way, the best clubs constantly monitor, measure and observe everything that is done, from the smallest detail to the largest, off the field as well as on. Although the individual members of the staff team and their work are constantly scrutinised, this is not carried out in a time-consuming and intrusive way that could undermine morale and confidence. A rounded methodology is employed to assess everything the club does; informed opinion, hard and soft data, feedback and observation are all used to guide decisions on people, systems and activity.

We have seen the value of relying on more holistic methods of measurement concerning staff effectiveness and activity impact. Although there exists a multidisciplinary environment inside elite football clubs, the best, including Bolton during the period to which we've alluded, strive to base their decisions on interdisciplinary approaches. Although difficult to do fully and constantly, clubs understand that this is the optimum way to make their work relate most closely to reality. And the reality they are focusing on is playing football. It is at the very best where we see football in science rather than sport science for football, and football coaching instead of coaching footballers. The danger with large resources and big teams of highly expert staff is that they will forget that their only goal is to do whatever they can to improve player performance and team results. The quality and rigour of the science, research support behind the sport psychology intervention or novelty of the coaching method are not important. Everything should be bent and shaped continually to meet the demands of the game, and the more skilled, knowledgeable and experienced the staff are, the greater the likelihood of this happening. It is only at clubs with poorly qualified and badly led staff that the real demands of producing winning football become secondary to the work being carried out. It is our belief that the ability to keep in mind that football performance is the most important factor to consider is what separates the best clubs from the rest. If the science, coaching, talent identification or welfare support does not improve the football, the solution is to change these support systems, not football!

2

GOVERNANCE AND TALENT IDENTIFICATION

Leadership

In view of recent government reviews on the governance of professional football in England (Whittingdale MP Chairman of Select Committee 2011 and Hugh Robertson Sports Minister January 2013) and in particular its ability to sustain itself financially, we were interested in looking at the structures in various countries to compare and analyse what impact this was having on the abilities of the professional clubs' youth development programmes to nurture and develop the professional footballers of tomorrow.

A strong theme that we see in European countries' football governance structures is that the national governing body is firmly in charge and appears to act with the best interests of the national teams first and clubs second. The consequences of this less complex structure are flexibility to change quickly to meet new challenges, joined-up thinking about their youth development programme, higher standards both in coach education and player output and ultimately more domestic players from which to choose their national teams (Elliot and Weedon, 2010).

The domestic rules and regulations in relation to youth development in many European countries facilitate the idea of the 'best working with the best', and we shall see how this thread weaves its way through the functions and processes involved in youth development in the following chapters.

Germany is a good case study to show as an example of how they dealt with changes to their youth development structure after two disappointing performances at international championships.

At the World Cup of 1998 in France, Germany performed poorly by their standards, losing 3–0 to Croatia in the quarter-finals and then performing even worse in the European Championships in 2000 – not getting past the group stage, which included England, who also didn't qualify from the same group. Germany's squad had an average age of 28.5, but only two players, Michael Ballack and Sebastian Deisler, were under the age of 24 and one was 39-year-old Lothar Matthäus. This sparked a root and branch review by the Deutscher Fussball-Bund (DFB), German football's national governing body, of their youth development structure. This included a visit to England to see how we had restructured our professional football youth development programme in 1997 known as 'The Charter for Quality.' This had been developed and implemented by Howard Wilkinson, who was then the Technical Director of the Football Association. The aim of the Charter was to develop a structure that would ultimately produce more English players for the Premier League and more players for the national team to choose from so we could compete more realistically in the major international competitions. However, the key difference was that the Football Association had to seek approval from the Professional Game Board, which is made up of key stakeholders in the football world (i.e. Premier League, Football League and Football Association). Often, matters voted upon were considered from a club point of view first and national team interest second.

Germany's new structure was implemented in 2002, and the appointment of Matthias Sammer as Technical Director in 2006 has given further impetus to their strategic plans. An early improvement to their plans was a professional club licensing scheme introduced in 2006 to categorize the professional clubs' youth development programmes dependent on strict criteria. The result of this restructuring is already bearing fruit with an unprecedented string of European titles over the recent years, winning the European Under-19 Championship in 2008, winning both the European Under-17 and European Under-21 Championships in 2009 and coming in runners up in the European Under-17 Championship in 2011.

The ultimate success of their new youth development programme saw their national team again compete in their 11th World Cup semi-final in South Africa. Christian Seifert, who has headed the German League since 2005, believes the rules that prevent a single investor from owning a majority in any one club "means you cannot have an owner who cares most of all about the success and financials of the club and who doesn't care so much about the national team."

We saw similar models and effects in Holland and France, where the Koninklijke Nederlandse Voetbalbond (KNVB – Royal Dutch Football Association – Holland's National Governing body) and Fédération Française de Football (FFF – national governing body in France) have for many years placed a focus on their youth development programmes but with their national teams being considered the primary importance. For instance, Clairefontaine in France is one of 12 national centres and is probably the most famous due to the players that have been developed there – players such as Thierry Henry, Louis Saha, Nicolas Anelka and more recently Hatem Ben Arfa to name but a few. It is based in the Ile de France region and has been operating as the National Centre since 1988. In Holland, only 14 clubs hold the Licence that enables them to recruit and develop players from under 9, and this, along with other rules, allows the best players to gravitate towards these licenced clubs.

Ownership

Professional football club ownership has taken on many changes since the start of the football league in 1888. They started life as mutual, membership clubs and then developed into limited companies, with shared ownership. The revenue now coming into professional football has never been greater and is attracting prospective owners from around the world. But what provision is being made to develop the stars of the future and the long-term good of the game? With around 52 English clubs going into some form of financial meltdown since the inception of the Premier League, we have seen the launch of Supporters Direct in 2000. Backed by the government, Supporters Trusts have become the saviour of last resort highlighted by the collapse of ITV Digital in 2002. However, the battle to financially compete against clubs with wealthy owners has seen several clubs fall back into the hands of individual businessmen.

If we look at Germany's football club ownership rules, we see that only traditional works teams such as Bayer's Bayer 04 Leverkusen and Volkswagen's VFL Wolfsburg can have the majority shareholding; otherwise, clubs cannot be owned by one single person, and 51% has to be owned by its members. This has been contested in recent years, and some accuse this rule of holding back investment in its professional game, but Franz Beckenbauer warned against being lured into the English model, as it will have the same long-term effect on its national teams as the English has suffered.

On 15 June 2010, Franz Beckenbauer commented about England's performance in the 2010 World Cup: "The English are being punished for the fact there are very few English players in the English Premier League clubs as they use better foreign players from all over the world."

Many of the clubs in Europe are sports clubs owned by their members, and therefore the responsibility is towards the local community. This develops a structure that is geared towards developing a local identity and opportunity for local talent. Barcelona is a good example of this type of ownership, with over 170,000 members, or 'socios' as they are known, and is reflected in their motto of *Més que un club* motto (English: More than a club). They underwent a complete change of leadership following the elections of June 2003, when Joan Laporta was elected as Chairman following years of poor management that had seen a net loss of €164m, the highest in the club's history, reported just after the election of that year. A group of associate members were able to conduct an upbeat-style election campaign and bring about changes to the way the organisation was to operate. The ability for the members to bring their board of directors to account allows the fans to be part of the process and appears to work very well. As of November 2010, membership of the club is no longer open to the public. Only close relatives of current and former FC Barcelona members can join the club, as well as previous members with at least a two-year history of membership. This ruling, however, will not apply to children under the age of 15. However, as always it is the vision, quality and commitment of the staff within a club that really make things happen, but having stable leadership increases the chance of success.

The status and influence of the Academy is often integral to the clubs' strategic aims, with many clubs having a representative at the boardroom level and technical board level. Two typical organisational charts adopted by foreign clubs in order to provide continuity and stability with their youth programmes are outlined below. You can see that the Academy Manager reports into either the Sports Director in the first chart and directly into the main Board in the second to avoid the obvious problems of change at the first team level.

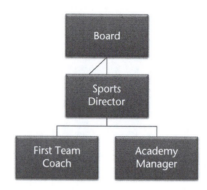

CHART 2.1

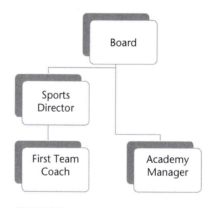

CHART 2.2

In July 2012, the new Elite Player Performance Plan (EPPP) developed by the Premier League was launched after three years of consultation and development. It is designed to address the fundamental issues of developing more home-grown talent for the Premier League and therefore more players for our international team to choose from. More detail follows in this chapter.

The new EPPP (Category 1) suggested the organisational chart below.

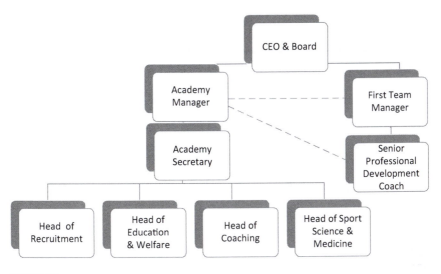

CEO & Board

Academy Manager

First Team Manager

Academy Secretary

Senior Professional Development Coach

Head of Recruitment

Head of Education & Welfare

Head of Coaching

Head of Sport Science & Medicine

CHART 2.3

The chart above is to recognise the functional relationship of the Academy Manager and the First Team Manager, but ultimately the Academy Manager is accountable to the CEO and Board. In the past, some clubs have appointed a particular Board member who is tasked with a focus on the Academy to report into the Board.

Academy Managers

At the coal face, most of the Academy Managers interviewed were former professional footballers, often having played for the club, with qualifications in other areas such as teaching and physical education. Stanley Brard at Feyenoord of Rotterdam fits this model, having played in the 1983/84 team with Johan Cruyff, which won both the Eredivisie and KNVB Cup. Stanley had become a youth and professional coach after his playing career finished. He coached at various clubs in Holland and in Japan before being invited back to take over the club's Academy operations. Having former players populate the coaching and other areas of the club reinforces local identity, continuity and a sense of family that fans and young players can relate to.

The current Academy Manager role in England has evolved into various guises, with each club making it fit their own needs. For instance, one leading Premier League club have adopted a business manager model whereby specialists in each function report into the Academy Manager, although those specialists have no previous Academy or professional football experience. Middlesbrough have a more traditional model whereby the Academy Manager is a qualified teacher and has a long coaching career, including involvement with the England schoolboy set-up before it transferred to the Football Association. Another club appointed someone with a scouting and recruitment background as their Academy Manager to boost their talent ID function. The job specification flexibility means they do not have to be qualified as an FA 'A' Licenced Coach, or Advanced Youth Award (launched in 2013), providing the Head of Coaching does hold these qualifications. Academy Managers who are actively involved with the coaching need to appoint an Operations Manager to take on most of the administrative day-to-day business. This flexibility is allowing clubs to build a structure that suits their own circumstances and will enrich the whole process of developing players. To support the administration function, Category 1 clubs have been offered a software programme that allows them to record and cross-reference many of their day-to-day activities so that in time the data can be analysed to inform practice.

Finance

In a recent report by the European Club Association in 2011, which reviewed professional football club Academies around Europe, they found that 50% of the clubs saw their Academies as a source to "create economic added value" and therefore a revenue stream and not a cost centre. Some Premier League clubs have evolved a business model that is almost making their Academies self-funding. This has developed from the loan system and the fees received. We see some clubs loan over 10 players out each season, charging various fees, which can be a win-win-win situation for the player to gain first team experience and build his profile, for the club to gain immediate return on investment and for the host club to gain the services of a player they would otherwise not afford. Much debate is now ensuing as the loan system is impacting on European qualification and relegation to such an extent that it is coming to the point where some sort of rules need to be put in place to prevent the perception that the bigger clubs are having too much influence over the integrity of the league.

The Premier League has already agreed to a £3 billion three-year domestic deal with Sky and BT Vision, and international rights close to being completed could add more than £2 billion more to the total. The clubs also generate large sums from the world's most expensive match day tickets. These large revenue streams cement the Premier Leagues title as the richest football competition in the world. These increases are also potentially insulating the clubs against the new Financial Fair Play rules introduced by UEFA from 2011/12 season, which we shall explore later.

Currently, most Premiership clubs will be investing less than 5% of their gross turnover on their youth development programmes, and this is becoming even less with the increase in revenue. The EPPP is going to provide substantial funding for each club ranging from a maximum of £775k for Category 1 clubs to £67k for Category 4 clubs, with funds from various sources including UEFA solidarity payments adding up to an estimated minimum funding for all participating clubs of £32 million in the first year. This funding is on a rising scale over a four-year period and dependent on which licence category the club has attained.

We consistently see that the European Academies' top clubs have on average bigger budgets than in England and invest far more of their gross turnover on their development programmes. This sends out a clear statement of intent that bolsters the community, its staff and players. For instance, AJ Auxerre have consistently invested up to 20% of their gross turnover, and they reached the Champions league in the 2010/11 season with three Academy graduates and consistently compete in European competitions. In France the budget for the 15 licenced clubs is between €2m and €7m. In Holland their budgets range from €1m to €7m but as a percentage of gross turnover are as much as 10%. On average, each Bundesliga club spends over €2.5m and has been doing so since 2008, which equates to around 8% of gross turnover. By far the biggest budget was Barcelona at €16m from a turnover of over €300m in 2009/10.

New rules

Over the past few years, FIFA and UEFA have been concerned about the movement of young players under the age of 18 from one country to another and the increase in expatriate (players playing in a country not of their origin) players filling teams. This has perhaps been exacerbated since the Bosman ruling in 1995 that ultimately allowed players over the age of 23 to move freely within the European community if their contracts had expired. In order to limit expatriate players flooding leagues and teams, to help maintain local identity and to keep the game's competitive integrity, two rules have had an impact on how clubs now view their youth development programmes. The first has been the 'home grown' quota: all 20 Premier League clubs must include eight home-grown players out of a squad of 25 at the start of each season but can have unlimited numbers of under-21 players in the squad. A Home Grown Player is defined as one who:

> Irrespective of his nationality or age has been registered with any club affiliated to the Football Association or the Football Association of Wales for a period, continuous or not, of three entire seasons or 36 months prior to his 21st birthday or the end of the season during which he turns 21.

Richard Scudamore (Premier League Chief Executive) commented, "We think it gives Clubs an extra incentive to invest in youth and we also think one of the benefits of that will be that it will help the England team."

The second ruling that has been implemented, having been passed by the UEFA executive committee in May 2010, is the financial fair play concept. One of its key objectives is to encourage clubs around Europe to invest in their youth development programmes. Financial fair play measures will be implemented over a three-year period, with the break-even assessment covering the financial years ending 2012 and 2013 and assessed in 2013/14 and starting with the assessment of all transfers and employee payables in the summer of 2011.

With these rule changes being anticipated, the Premier League has for the past three years been developing a new youth development structure called the Elite Player Performance Plan (EPPP) to build on the initial work that Howard

Wilkinson had developed, i.e. the Charter for Quality. This was launched on 1 July 2012, and has six fundamental principles:

1   Increase the number and quality of home-grown players gaining professional contracts and playing first team football at the highest level
2   Create more coaching and playing time
3   Improve coaching provision
4   Implement a system of effective measurement and quality assurance
5   Positively influence strategic investment into the Academy system, demonstrating value for money
6   Seek to implement significant gains in every aspect of player development

Each professional club that runs a youth development programme in England has had to submit an application via a document called the Audit Tool to determine which category they will qualify for and subsequent funding available. Category 1 clubs will have the most comprehensive criteria and will be investing a minimum of £2.3m per year to cater to the holistic needs of the players and not least the full-time education and welfare commitment needed to facilitate more coaching time from age 12. Category 2, 3 and 4 clubs will spend considerably less and will have a reduced criteria to meet and therefore less funding assistance. All clubs will be subject to an independent audit to gain their licence and determine their category status, and this will be an ongoing process every three years unless a club requests an interim audit for a change of category. The intention of the EPPP is to give English players a far more professional pathway to a career in professional football, produce more players with the ability to play in the Premier League and give our England teams more players of international quality to choose from.

The initial funding for the EPPP as mentioned previously is for four years and will amount to a substantial financial increase across youth development in the professional game.

Vision and strategy

Often, the most successful clubs in England and Europe are those with a clear vision and philosophy that has been in place for many years and can be likened to their 'DNA' or identity, and we see this most visibly at Manchester United, Ajax and Barcelona, as well as many other successful clubs. Since the 1950s, Ajax has had a style of play that is based on attacking and expansive football. Rinus Michels, a former Ajax player, became their manager in 1965 and is credited with the introduction of 'total football,' which allowed players the freedom to be multifunctional. This apparently very fluid approach has been formalised with the numbers on the player's shirts being given distinct job descriptions in the context of the game. That is to say, the Ajax system can appear quite fluid but is really a complex series of set plays with players' roles and responsibilities defined by the number they wear so that each player becomes familiar with the pictures he will see when in possession of the ball in various parts of the pitch. The young players are developed over many years of practice so that each player understands what their roles and responsibilities are within the team structure dependent on the number they are wearing. New managers/coaches who are appointed are expected to manage the philosophy and enhance the values and beliefs. Rinus Michels also had a great effect on Barcelona and their philosophy. He was very focused on developing a culture.

> The culture of the club is the overall vision supported by everyone in the club, from players to staff to Chairman . . . everyone realizes that if they are to remain at the club they will have to respect certain rules . . . the more extreme and recognisable the culture within the club, the better it works.
>
> Rinus Michels (2001)

Since the 70s, Barcelona have had a string of Dutch coaches but Johan Cruyff's influence from 1988 to 1995 has cemented the 'tiki-taka' (short passing) rondos (repeated musical composition) style of play we see Barcelona portray with great success today. Again the philosophy has been engrained in the youth programme, and the clarity and consistency has allowed players of world class to emerge, such as Andres Iniesta, Xavi Hernandez, Carles Puyol and many more. This style of play puts a lot of responsibility on the technical, tactical and psychological elements of the players' development.

Hernandez sums up the Barcelona approach to development:

> When you arrive at Barcelona the first thing they teach you is to think, think, think quickly . . . some youth Academies worry about winning we worry about education. Rondo, Rondo, Rondo (keep ball exercises played with a rhythm and a style) it is the best exercise of all . . . you learn to take responsibility with the ball.

We often find in England that with each new managerial change the club's philosophy changes, and this lack of clarity and consistency resonates throughout the club, causing mistrust, turnover of staff and fear to fully commit (Gilmore and Gilson, 2007). The effect on the development of young players is that they get confused by mixed messages and this environment hinders their progression as footballers. The new EPPP is designed so that clubs will ask these fundamental questions and add clarity to their plans as an Academy and as a business.

The clear main objective for all Academies is to produce players for their first team and clubs who appear to be happy if one player per season graduates from the Academy into the first team squad. But how many players does the industry need each season? There are around 2,800 professional footballers playing in the top four divisions of the English leagues. Each season roughly a third are out of contract, of which around 350 get new contracts at their existing clubs. This appears to leave around 550 possible places. However, these 550, along with around 750 scholars (trainees who start on a two-year full-time contract at age 16, which includes

12 hours of academic education and a full-time training programme with the aim of becoming a professional footballer) graduate each year and foreign players, will all be competing for professional contracts. The attrition rate for young professionals ages 18–21 is around 85%. Clearly it is a competitive industry, and the average career span is eight years. It is very difficult to put an exact number on what the industry needs, but new players gaining a place in the first team squads of professional clubs would appear to be less than 200 per year. Obviously clubs need to fill teams below the first team so that players can develop in realistic environments, but it does add costs. One suggestion put forward by the French Football Federation was to extend the time their elite players spent at the 12 national centres to 18 years old. Currently 11 centres develop the boys until they are 15. Clairefontaine are the exception and develop their boys for 3 years from 13 to 16. This would allow the clubs to make more informed decisions and not incur as much cost. They estimated that they need around 100 new professionals each season to replenish stocks in their two professional leagues. In Holland, there are 38 professional teams with first team squads of around 20 players and a total number of professionals around 800. The KNVB are conducting detailed research asking fundamental questions such as: When is a player part of professional football? How many professional first team games does he have to play? How many years must he have played in an Academy? The answers have implications for governance and also for other areas like talent identification.

We will now turn to this topic because in many ways what an Academy can do depends very much on the talent it can attract, retain and develop. A club that is poorly led, lacks a vision and suffers from poor governance will struggle even if it is fortunate enough to have highly talented young players. In our research we found that the best clubs benefitted from excellent governance and well-resourced, planned and rigorous systems of player recruitment.

Talent identification and recruitment

Before we look at our field-based evidence, we wanted to look briefly at some of the academic literature and what scientific evidence is there that might point us in the right direction towards talent ID. Professor Dave Collins, former Performance Director at UK Athletics and now Professor of Coaching and Performance at University of Central Lancashire, was tasked with asking some of the big questions around talent ID and development for our Great Britain athletes. He suggests that even genetic tests appear not valid as an indicator for potential. When you try to manipulate genetic engineering, only 1 in 10 are successful in horse racing, but big returns make it cost effective. They trained Red Rum as a sprinter, but he went on to win three Grand Nationals! He also points out that early potential is not a good indicator for future development, and a good example of this was Mark Lewis-Francis, who ran a 100m in 9.9 seconds at the age of 16 but never improved on that. Scotland's greatest feat in football was their under-17s getting to the world final in 1989 but only two players made lasting professional careers, one of which most notably was Paul Dickov. Professor Collins warns that the biggest problem we have is that we often get sucked into choosing talent based on performance, but that often means choosing early developers and not potential. Bloom (1985) suggests the emphasis should be on development and not talent identification – it's a numbers game, lots of practice and large participation within a pyramid.

So what should we look for?

> "The various traits slowly appear and differentiate over time . . . infancy, adolescence and even adulthood will see latent components undergoing various transformations."
>
> (Simonton, 2001)

> "There is no magic wand to talent ID."
>
> (Lumpkin et al., 1999)

The New Zealand Sports Academy in 2003 published its research conclusions into what they saw as desirable attributes and common themes in elite athletes and Olympic champions:

- Very active as children, doing around 25 hours of play and activity per week
- Active in more sports than those who didn't make it or next best, had specialised later and had a relatively slow career development
- Motivated by intrinsic motives such as the joy of the sport, the training and gradual improvement versus extrinsic motives such as winning and medals
- Enjoyed immense support from their family and little pressure from them to succeed
- Grew up in families with other siblings
- Were more independent of friends
- Were more interested in local than offshore heroes as role models
- Were independent and creative

Olympic champions

Research into Olympic winners has identified the following key success factors as being most common to most successful Olympians:

- Dedication and persistence
- Support of family, friends and coaches
- Love of the sport, training programmes and facilities
- Innate talent
- Competitiveness
- Financial support

The rules that govern recruitment have been quite different in Europe to facilitate this idea of the 'best with the best' for many years (Littlewood et al., 2011).

Clubs who invest and meet the national association's highest criteria can recruit players from anywhere in their country, and there are compensation packages to allow this to happen. For example, in Holland the buying club currently pays under €15k for each year a boy has been with the selling club from the age of 12, and there are also performance and sell-on clauses built into the compensation package.

This has been in contrast to England, who via the Charter for Quality rules implemented in 1997 imposed a one-hour journey time for under-9–11 and a one and one-half hour time for under-12–16 boys. However, this has now changed under the new EPPP rules. Clubs who attain Category 1 status are now able to recruit from anywhere in England from age 12 from the 2013/14 season. However, the clear message on this issue is that foreign clubs either impose an unwritten limit or there is a club policy to recruit within similar travel time limits as England for the reasons of attendance, keeping a local identity, reluctance to get involved in the added costs and resources required to cater to holistic needs when outcomes are so uncertain and the moral judgement of taking players out of their home environment too soon, which could have long-term psychological consequences.

Many of the European clubs visited recruited local players up to under 14 and then started to search countrywide and then Europe-wide at 16 to fit within the UEFA rules. All the clubs invested in a structured scouting network and supported that with computer systems to keep data and to track players. We see that a good number of elite players are emanating from Africa and South America, where socio-economic conditions still exist that encourage street football, and the dream of becoming a professional footballer is a clear motivation for many. This has prompted many clubs to invest scouting resources into these regions of the world. As part of this network, we see some big European clubs forge formal links with football clubs in countries that can make the transition into Europe easier due to their immigration laws. For example, we see that France has strong working relations with many North African countries, which is a legacy of their colonial past but has had a big impact on their football talent pool – for instance, the impact that players such as Nicolas Anelka, Zinedine Zidane and Youri Djorkaeff have had on French national football, culminating in winning the World Cup in 1998.

One of the recruitment staff at Barcelona gave an interesting anecdote as to why they like to have some foreign players in their older squads:

> The Japanese people have a real liking for tuna fish and this has led to stocks around the world to fall and the price to rise therefore the Japanese decided to farm their own. However what they found was that because they weren't in the wild and subject to the stress of predators the meat became less palatable. By trial and error, they discovered that by introducing sharks into their habitat it stressed the tuna and the meat became high quality again but had to accept that they might lose up to 10% of the stock.

Another strategy we see clubs employ is running 'shadow squads' – groups that run parallel with the main squads from under-9 all the way through to under-18.

The purpose of these squads is to cater to the late developers, and the squads are often made up of boys whose birthdates are in the second half of the year, a phenomenon known as birth bias or relative age affect. This has been highlighted by authors such as Malcolm Gladwell (2008) in his book *Outliers*, and repeated statistics have told us for many years that around 60% of professional footballers in England are born in the first quartile of the school year, i.e. September to December. Many academics (e.g. Van Yperen, 2009; Reilly et al., 2000) and sports professionals have looked at this issue, as it is not unique to football and applies to almost any sport and even academia, but there appear to be no easy answers. It does suggest that opportunity plays a big part in development, and what can be mistaken for talent can often be early maturation and opportunities to practice and compete that help players initially but often leaves coaches, players and parents disappointed as the players fail to fulfil expectations. As we alluded to earlier, there is strong evidence to suggest it is those athletes who have that capacity to be persistent and look to be more task orientated with their development that eventually reach elite levels and become the champions.

Because many of the clubs in Europe are sports clubs, they have an amateur section which acts like a shadow squad, and we see this working well at AJ Auxerre. They place their second and third tier players at age 16 into a sports college similar to the college programme in England, but the relationship is more formal and monitored. Bacary Sagna, who now plays for Arsenal and was part of the AJ Auxerre team of 2005 that won the French Cup, is a good example of this strategy working.

Some clubs have very organised structures of national feeder clubs at various levels, and this was very much part of the recruitment strategy in Holland and Germany. They were linked into amateur clubs around the immediate area to help with local scouting but were also linked into clubs around the country to help broaden their network. These associations went all the way to the professional level. When the KNVB introduced their licencing scheme for Academy clubs, they also encouraged those clubs who were not granted a licence to build relationships with the bigger clubs for this two-way process, whereby the non-licenced Academy clubs are able to receive relatively small initial payments for any young talent they may have but would receive more as the player achieved greater success and would also be given first refusal on getting the player back if he didn't make the grade. It also worked on other levels such as exchange of ideas and resources, keeping costs to a minimum for the smaller clubs. Research undertaken by the KNVB also proved that most of the best young players were being developed by the bigger clubs in Holland, and therefore this new arrangement created a win–win situation for both parties. For example, Feyenoord have a close relationship with another professional club in Rotterdam, Excelsior, who have traditionally played below the Eredivisie. This link allows Feyenoord access to their best young players but also allows them to loan players back to them for first team experience. This has been very successful over the years with Thomas Buffel and Salomon Kalou, who were both subsequently sold for millions of euros. Excelsior also gained promotion to the Eredivisie in 2010 with 10 players on loan from Feyenoord.

We often hear that any development programme is a numbers game, and the more populated the foundation levels the more chance there is for elite talent to emerge at the top end. UK Sport was tasked with finding the best talent to compete at the 2012 Olympics and Paralympics and underlines the idea of numbers being a significant factor in talent ID. Since its inception in 2006, the UK Talent Team have assessed over 7,000 individuals from across Britain using initiatives such as Pitch-2Podium, which is giving young footballers who have not quite made a professional career the chance to transfer their skills into an Olympic sport. As a result of this and other initiatives, over 50 athletes have been given the opportunity to further enhance their skills in high-performance environments and are now on the Olympic and Paralympic development programmes. These athletes who are striving for their own success are playing a vital role in applying pressure upwards on those already at the top of their sport and increasing the strength and depth of the world-class talent pool within the British high-performance system. The programmes have already produced 54 international medallists (at senior and junior levels), including eight world championship, three European Championship and nine World Cup medals. Helen Glover (GB Rowing) perhaps epitomised these achievements by winning silver at the World Championships in 2010. Helen achieved this feat within four years of being discovered and first stepping into a rowing boat. She then went on to become the world and Olympic champion in the women's coxless pair in 2012.

We found evidence to support this notion of population of the region where clubs were situated being a significant factor towards finding talent. Barcelona are situated in the fifth most populated area within the EU, and Clairefontaine recruit from the most densely populated area of France, Ile de France, which includes Paris. Ajax are situated in Amsterdam, which boasts the largest populated city in Holland. Another key indicator is that the clubs are situated in areas where there is very little or no competition for the talented boys and can therefore place the best with the best and not be watered down by competition for the same talent, which is what we often find in England, especially in areas where there are many Premier League clubs such as London and the North West.

Many of the clubs visited have a set of criteria that clarifies what the scouts should be looking for in young talent and is often abbreviated into an acronym. For instance, TABS = Technique, Attitude, Balance, Speed or TEAM = Technique, Education (football), Athleticism, Mentality. The most famous one, however, is Ajax's SPIT = Speed, Personality, Insight, Technique. They define this further by stating that they believe Speed and Personality cannot be changed greatly and that these things are mainly genetically programmed, but with lots of practice and consistent messages, neuro-plasticity up to the age of 20 allows new things to be learnt more easily; therefore, Technique and Insight (understanding the tactics of the game) can be developed to elite levels. B. Malina (2006 Lecture at JMU) suggested that muscular mesomorph body types are more likely to mature into the quick, powerful athletes required for football, e.g. Wayne Rooney, Michael Owen. Ajax subsequently turn their acronym round to TIPS in terms of the focus areas for development.

The use of sport science assessments and medical examinations alongside football benchmarking has become more prevalent in recent years in England and appears to be catching on in Europe. This is obviously designed to minimise risks of failure and over time perhaps gather data that will give a greater insight to key performance indicators for elite footballers. The battery of field tests usually undertaken to measure speed, strength, power and endurance are the standard 10- and 30-metre sprints, agility 'T' test, Jump Mat test and 'bleep' test. Although some would argue about why these tests are performed at prepubescent ages because of the lack of physiological elements such as testosterone, they are really informing the coach that the most productive years for trainability of major physical functions are yet to come. Nike have conducted some very detailed physical research via the SPARQs programme, which looked into top performing athletes and suggested that if athletes wish to attain elite levels they need to be in the top quartile of their sport from a physical perspective by the time they are 18 years old.

> Better athletes, better players: steady progression of the rating by playing level: U18 players who rate greater than 69 are 7 times as likely as age-group matched peers of playing for a Premier League Academy.
> (Nike UK football census and analytics, 18 March 2012)

The race towards gathering data has quite naturally emphasised those elements of the game that can easily be measured and quantified and therefore more tangible when justifying costs. Over time this will better inform the industry to understand where a child's development is within his biological peers' norms as opposed to his chronological peers. This in turn will allow clubs to be more patient and perhaps give a greater chance to the late developer. Testing appears to become more sophisticated when recruiting boys from under 14 upwards. Examples of this sophistication are taking x-rays of wrists and comparing them to bones of a standard atlas to determine final height within 2cm, checking school reports for academic ability and social behaviour and body laser machines for anthropometric measurements.

The psychological area is possibly the last frontier to be formally assessed and developed despite many coaches and managers expressing its importance (Reilly et al., 2000).

There still seems to be a reluctance to address this critical function, and clubs generally relied on informal feedback from staff, especially coaches looking at player behaviours in and around the training ground and their responses to tasks and informal conversations.

The EPPP is now demanding that clubs put in place a psychological support programme and that coaches, when planning, include psychological outcomes in their sessions. This will start to formalise clubs' focus on traits and behaviours that scouts should look for within the players and that coaches will perhaps test during coaching sessions and matches. Putting players into calculated trauma situations, for instance, playing with one player less in the team or playing against bigger stronger boys can start to test the commitment and persistence of young players.

However, by taking a slightly different approach to the issue of identifying talent in young players, it is possible to refer to research from a range of sports at elite level that indicates the best performers use mental skills more than their less elite counterparts. This has been reported by a number of studies (Bota, 1993; Cumming and Hall, 2002; Wilson, 1999) and includes skills related to goal setting, imagery, use of intrinsic motivation strategies, focusing, arousal regulation and pre-performance routines. These young elite players were also more skilled at using appropriate coping strategies and at dealing with setbacks and the demands of training. The most interesting conclusion from this body of work is that mental skills in young athletes seem to be genetically influenced and related to social cognitive factors, the most important being levels of self-determination (intrinsic motivation).

If, as some evidence suggests, that much of the psychological profile of a player is 'hard wired,' particularly with the perceptual motor abilities such as reaction speed, visual acuity, kinaesthetic awareness and timing, it appears that these are inherited. More promisingly, mental skills can be developed and improved with the right type of training, and this should be a feature of development work with young elite players. The improvements in these skills and qualities can be measured over time by the use of semi-structured interviews, sport psychology questionnaires and observation. As Gould (2001) has suggested, it seems that mental skills and motivation do not remain stable from youth stages to adulthood; therefore, great care should be taken with the use and interpretation of data captured during this period.

Talent identification is more problematic from a psychological perspective than almost any other area of predicting and nurturing expert performance. This means that the focus should always be more on providing opportunities for young players to acquire new skills in game-based scenarios than attempting to identify a rigid set of criteria against which players will be assessed. Measurements can be made; however, we need to respect the complexity of child development, its dynamic and fluid nature and that the talent of the early achiever can be surpassed by the often more persistent and self-motivated improvements of the late developer.

Ricardo Kaka (AC Milan and Brazilian footballer) expresses his physical development and how this galvanised his mentality in this quote:

> My bones were 2 years slow in developing . . . when I was 12, I physically looked 10 and that was the way it was until I was 15 or 16 when things normalised. Sao Paulo worked with me to build me up, but we just had to wait and when the time came and I filled out. It was hard, but I learned from it. I learned to fight for what I wanted.

Smith and Christensen (1995) developed the Athletic Coping Skills Inventory (ACSI-28), which was designed to assess seven psychological skills that athletes use to manage their sports performance. These seem to be a much better predictor of athletic success than physical skills. These consisted of coping with adversity, coachability, concentration, confidence and achievement motivation, goal setting and mental preparation, peaking under pressure and freedom from worry.

What is clear is that the foundation phase is the crucial phase for laying down movement patterns relevant to football. Dr Danny Mielke, the author of *Soccer Fundamentals* from Eastern Oregon University, is an expert on motor development and termed the years 7 to 12 as "the period of critical readiness." This means it is the period when children are most receptive to learning psychomotor skills. It is also becoming the most critical period for professional football clubs to recruit talent. Several reasons create this urgency: one is that players cannot sign an official contract until they are in their under-9 year. Second, compensation costs are minimal when one boy transfers across to another club. The cost of compensation increases significantly past 12 years of age and is where UEFA have fixed their starting age for compensation when a boy transfers across borders to another country.

Trying to spot talent at the early ages and then confirm it is a complex task that carries no guarantees of long-term success. Therefore, having large numbers who have been chosen for their mentality, physical potential and football ability placed into a development programme that creates a safe learning environment and provides opportunity for a variety of experiences will have the best chance of success.

Based on the research and our applied experiences, we would make the following recommendations:

1   The interests of clubs should coincide with those of the national governing bodies to improve youth development. Where this does not happen, clubs and national teams will suffer problems in terms of the quality and quantity of players produced.

2   Youth development will be improved where clubs' ownership models include local representation and involvement from the supporters.

3   Clubs will do best when they have a clear vision and philosophy that impacts all aspects of the club, including youth development. Four of the most important aspects to be affected by this are playing style, recruitment policies, coaching practices and financial systems.

4   The best clubs take great care to use scientific measures and to craft knowledge from coaches and other staff to identify the best talent. Every effort is made to use a wide range of measures and to collect data over a prolonged period of time, with the emphasis very clearly on potential for football performance.

5   Clubs and national governing bodies should do all in their power to ensure that talent pools are not diluted. The best should be able to face the best; young players, especially after the age of 14, improve most when placed in a highly competitive and supportive environment, where they can learn and grow alongside equally talented players.

6   Academy Managers can be from a range of former professional backgrounds. More important is that they are supported by the club and have job security that allows them to build systems and plan for the future with confidence. The best clubs fight hard to maintain this level of stability in the Academy, irrespective of first team changes.

7   Good governance, optimum talent identification and player recruitment require a sound culture. The Academy director and staff must be cultural architects; they must help to build an elite performance culture through all aspects of their roles.

3

EDUCATING THE WHOLE PERSON

A major part of the holistic development of players at professional football clubs is being able to manage young players' education and welfare needs. This mainly revolves around facilitating time for the boys to be coached through academic and welfare support. This has been a key area that English clubs have grappled with since the Charter for Quality was introduced in 1997, but very few have addressed it to the level of foreign clubs. This has had a real effect on training times and frequency and therefore development. However, the EPPP is making it part of the criteria for Category 1 clubs to provide a structured programme that caters to the holistic needs of the boys. In comparison, all the centres and clubs we visited have a good working relationship with educational establishment(s) that allows the boys a flexible curriculum timetable to pursue a dual pathway of education and football development. Aspire (Doha City), for instance, have the school on-site, but usually the school is within a short distance of the training centre and mini buses are used to ferry the boys. Barcelona, for example, have an agreement that the boys have a summer timetable all year round that allows them out of school at 2pm. Bayern Munich have arrangements with three schools for their boys from 11 years of age, depending on the boys' academic ability, to be placed in one of these schools. They felt it was very important that the young boys were placed in schools commensurate with their academic ability so that they are not demotivated in that environment, which can then spill over into their football world.

All the centres offered extra individual academic support via part-time tutors to give the boys every chance of passing their grades and minimise the risk of conflict that could be detrimental to the boys' football development.

With regards to accommodation for the boys 14 and older, most centres have a mix-and-match arrangement where they have some on-site accommodation and some off-site accommodation in the form of home stays and club-owned flats for the older boys. Feyenoord and Bayern Munich have a small accommodation block but prefer the players to travel from home, and the older boys are placed in club-owned flats. AJ Auxerre and Aspire, for instance, have all their full-time boys on-site, but AJ Auxerre separate the boys by age group into different buildings starting at under 17.

All the centres stressed the importance of having the right type of person(s) to operate the on-site and off-site club accommodation arrangements.

In terms of holistic development, Dr Larson at the Aspire Academy in Qatar said some very interesting things around the holistic development of the boys:

- Create a culture of performance both on and off the pitch via goal setting supported by quantifiable evidence.
- Try to balance enough sport to develop but not so much they lose desire or focus. The new training timetable has been reduced by one session per week to eight per week after consultation with key staff.
- Go from a fun environment to a competitive environment over the time of their development (i.e. from ages 6–11 fun to ages 12–18 competitive).
- *"Don't focus on the score; learn a little more."*
- Team building is critical for long-term development. Living together is not necessarily conducive to building a good team spirit, so it has to be promoted by staff values and behaviour.
- Build into the curriculum a life skills programme and the value of leadership.

Psychological well-being and dealing with pressure

Well-being has become something of a fashionable term of late. Rarely a day passes without someone from national government or an expert in academia telling us that a new measure has been developed that will assist the population in attaining greater levels of mental well-being and psychological health. In contrast, in the world of professional football, there is much talk about performance mind-sets and mental toughness, and little mention of well-being. When we consider the activities of staff rather than the words they use to describe their roles, it becomes very apparent that, especially at youth levels, football clubs are carrying out lots of work aimed at improving the psychological health of their players. The clearest example is through the work of welfare officers and chaplains (where these exist). For these individuals there is an ethical and moral commitment to help the players deal with the myriad of challenges they face in their time at the club. Outside of this, the work of the sport psychologist where one is employed, and even the support from physiotherapy and medical staff, can have a very significant positive impact on the psychological health of the young players. Although all of these individuals can play a major role in this area, we believe that the best clubs recognise that their coaches can be the most influential in this regard.

There are two main ways that coaches can affect the psychological well-being of players. First, they can support the player off the field. This can extend to their involvement with the young person in relation to family support and in dealing with conflict with peers and other support staff. Although welfare staff are usually highly skilled at helping players with advice around lifestyle matters, coaches are ideally placed, given the high level of contact they have, to convey appropriate messages and encourage sound lifestyle choices in their players. This was carried out with great care at several of the clubs we have worked at and studied. Notable examples would be at Barcelona, Feyenoord and Bolton Wanderers, where coaches were encouraged to see their role as being about the whole care of the players, from competitive play to lifestyle, and clear structures were in place to formalise this dimension. For example, frequent and regular meetings were organised that involved all Academy staff at which the main agenda item was player welfare on and off the field of play. Formal reports were kept and made accessible to all staff to ensure complete sharing of information where it was possible and desirable to assist the young player.

Second, the coach will usually have the major role in player preparation for training and matches. With the exception of Feyenoord in our European sample, few clubs at this level had full-time or even part-time sport psychologists to help with this type of work. In our discussions with coaches and Academy Directors, we heard how they were becoming more aware and knowledgeable about the way in which various performance-related psychological factors impacted on both well-being and competitive achievement. One of the words we heard most often at all of the clubs we visited was *pressure*. This term is rarely mentioned in most academic sport psychology textbooks or research articles. This may seem a strange omission, until a closer inspection reveals that sport psychologists are also very interested in this topic, although they have broken it down into several different but related concepts and constructs.

Typically, sport psychologists have described pressure in terms of the concepts of stress, coping and anxiety. The reason not to use the word *pressure* is because, it is argued, it is not a sufficiently precise term; it does not allow us to easily differentiate pressure that causes negative outcomes from the type that is good for us.

In some ways this problem has also been seen in definitions of stress. Despite the description of Selye (1956) (who was the first individual to describe stress from a psychological perspective) that we could encounter positive stress, which he labelled eustress, or negative stress, referred to as distress, the generally held view is that stress is to be avoided at all costs. This rather confusing view is not very useful in areas like high level sport, where research suggests performers encounter high levels of stress of both the positive and destructive variety. Arguably, this has led to a number of unfortunate and unintended consequences. First, coaches and others are aware of the value of placing young players in situations of high stress to help them to develop the skill to cope with it. They do this because, not unreasonably, they anticipate that as the players progress in their careers they will face greater demands and increased stress. They want them to be able to withstand this, and even be able to enjoy and thrive in this environment of heightened stress. They hope that through the work they do with the young players that, eventually, the experience they have on, say, achieving reserve team football will be one with moments of eustress rather than crushing distress. This will help the players to meet the higher performance expectations at this level and maintain good levels of psychological well-being.

Second, the players are aware through their own experiences of learning and progression that, as they move up the ladder, everything becomes more pressured or, as we are suggesting here, more laden with stress. This means that they already have an understanding from their lived experience that stress is not all bad, and indeed it is part of the job. It accompanies learning new things and facing difficult challenges. So, to summarise, the coaches and players at youth levels often have a more complete and nuanced understanding about stress and its effects, positive or otherwise, than do some psychologists it seems. If coaches are going to be convinced to alter their approach to working with young players, it is important that we take seriously their opinions. It is not good enough to dismiss these as not based on sound empirical evidence or robust theories where it is clear that practices have resulted in success. In this case that means young players acquiring the skills and personal psychological qualities (i.e. character) to deal effectively with the greater levels of stress at professional first team levels. This will also help them in terms of well-being, because progressing and dealing successfully with the challenges of competitive play are central to the lives of young players. Individual feelings of sound well-being and the psychology of performance are inextricably connected; helping the development of one is very likely to impact on the strength of the other.

Another important psychological concept that influences player well-being is that of anxiety. This concept can be viewed in a number of different ways depending on the theoretical orientation being used. For example, cognitive approaches to sport psychology have tended to describe this phenomenon in terms of competitive anxiety. This has traditionally been viewed as something to be avoided because it has been reported to interfere with successful performance. Sport psychologists will often recommend various mental skills, like imagery, performance routines or goal setting, to help manage the symptoms of competitive anxiety to remove or reduce their impact. The main problem, though, is that despite many researchers adopting this perspective (until more recently when it was accepted that sometimes competitive anxiety could facilitate performance), coaches and players have expressed a more ambivalent view about competitive anxiety and its likely effect in football. Evidence based on extensive applied work in football, especially at higher levels, indicates that some players deliberately ramp up their feelings of anxiety before they perform because past experiences tell them that this emotional state is linked to their best performances and results. Conversely, others know that they will struggle if they feel anxious before competing; usually most players, especially older and more experienced ones, will already have various ways to try to control their anxiety and combat any deleterious effects before and during the match itself.

It is not uncommon for experienced youth coaches to decide to escalate feelings of competitive anxiety in their teams or with individual players because experience has led them to believe that this can increase motivation, persistence and focus. Of course, the highly skilled coach understands that this same strategy applied to another group of players, before different game situations or after a period of confidence-draining results and performances, could be very counterproductive.

In one sense we could argue that the approach to anxiety reflects the importance coaches and others place on player well-being and performance. Teaching players to understand their anxiety so that they can accept it as part of learning and change, or on other occasions use mental skills techniques to control it, is a vital life skill. It also happens to be essential for players to ensure they can succeed in the ever more stressful environment of first team professional football.

It was evident at several clubs that a holistic perspective was being adopted towards players' psychological well-being. Support staff, and coaches most especially, told us that they did not see a strict separation between players' mental states on and off the field of play. To them, the knowledge acquired by players in matches and training helped the development of important life skills; these help the young person to achieve in all areas of their lives. We noticed that at some clubs (e.g. Feyenoord and Ajax) young players were clearly encouraged to use the psychological skills, knowledge and qualities they learned in competitive football to help them progress in their education and to be able to deal more effectively with other demands like family, social contact and time management.

We could argue that the craft knowledge of the coaches is more truly empirical than the research and theories about competitive anxiety in sport. Knowledge derived from practice suggests that competitive anxiety has always been seen as something capable of crushing individuals and teams, leaving them full of doubt, lacking in confidence and incapable of carrying out good decision making. At other times coaches and players use a number of means to psyche themselves up. This involves deliberately trying to increase levels of mental stimulation, which in turn generate more intense feelings of anxiety and motivation in order to get enhanced performances from players. Unfortunately, many sport psychologists have criticised this behaviour as always inappropriate and likely to be associated with poor performances. The evidence from the real world does not support this. A more empirical and balanced account would help matters greatly and allow an understanding of when to avoid or reduce anxiety, and where the challenge is to embrace anxiety or even increase its level.

Implications

There are a number of important factors that emerge from the consideration of stress, coping, competitive anxiety and existential anxiety for player well-being and performance. These are equally of concern to coaches, sport psychologists and other support staff who may be working closely with the young players.

First, it seems that the traditional way of dealing with and understanding these concepts in youth football has much merit. Whilst this should please those who think that the old ways are best, it is a little more complicated than that. But then it should be since we are talking about the complexities of the mind and the fact of individual uniqueness and contextual variation!

Our research and applied engagement over many years with Academy coaches at some of the best clubs in the world reveal a common pattern in dealing with stress and anxiety. First of all, we have observed how coaches and other support staff attempt to create conditions where young players are subject to increasing levels of stress and anxiety to prepare them for the realities of first team professional football. There are a number of ways to do this, such as through use of simulated events or by deliberately psyching up players. However, in the best environments, such as Feyenoord, Ajax and Bayern Munich, this was done by developing high levels of personal responsibility in the players. In more familiar football terminology, this is sometimes referred to as pride. The task facing the coaches and other staff is to inculcate greater levels of personal and professional pride in the players – in what they do, how they do it and how they are perceived by others. This is encouraged by setting targets for the players and through developing expectations around acceptable standards of performance. This does not mean only on the field of play in matches and training, but is about everything young footballers must attend to in their lives.

Academy Directors were keen to tell us that they viewed their roles encouraging players to grow in professional pride, and the capacity to take greater levels of responsibility for their own actions, as a moral obligation. This was about helping young people become more autonomous, self-disciplined and responsible. Staff spoke about how this could impact on performance and motivation. Equally, they also stressed that this form of education was the right thing to do given how few players make the grade beyond youth levels. For example, one education and welfare officer at a very successful club mentioned that without being committed to the broader goal of teaching players to become self-directed and responsible individuals, he would be unable to justify his job from an ethical standpoint. He added that although most parents quite naturally expected their sons to be successful at the club, the reality was that only about 5% of the total intake would have a career as professional players. If this was the success rate in a school, it would most likely be closed down. Given this unfortunate but unavoidable reality, it is therefore very important that all learning the players experience is oriented towards giving them skills and knowledge that can be used throughout their lives.

The optimum conditions for this to occur are to be found where an Academy culture is totally oriented towards supporting players to take personal responsibility for their own learning and progress. This is not in any way an easy or soft option. At Ajax we heard how the staff took great care to outline, explain and reaffirm the standards expected to make the next level. The young players were continually educated to understand that it will be by their own efforts and desire that they will be able to meet these standards.

This approach to education, one where personal responsibility is encouraged, especially during the frequently experienced uncomfortable moments of elite performance sport, will contribute to the stress and anxiety experienced. Of course, as will be argued in Chapter 7 on sport psychology, this type of existential anxiety will be felt only by those prepared to confront a challenge and become willing to accept responsibility. It is also true that this type of anxiety is a good sign, because according to existential psychology, we feel anxiety only about things we care about. Once we are no longer committed to some course of action or an event, it loses meaning for us, and we are incapable of feeling anxiety about its outcome. It is because of this relationship between responsibility, choice, meaning and anxiety that the experienced high-quality youth coaches we have encountered do not automatically see anxiety as a negative feature. Indeed, they tend to understand it as a positive sign – as evidence that youth players still care deeply about what they are doing because it remains something they deeply wish for and hope to achieve. This is a lesson that will help young people become better players now and contribute to their lives when their football careers are over.

This deeper and more psychologically informed view about player welfare and well-being is in tune with the performance philosophy at the best Academies. It is interesting to note that very few of these clubs had sport psychologists in place. They had built up these views over time and by careful reflection on practice in all aspects of the clubs' work. Given this commitment to a broader and more psychologically grounded approach to player welfare, sport psychologists working in these cultures must take great care to consider how existential anxiety relates to players' motivation and achievement. They should not equate anxiety of this type to something that is always negative, as has largely been the case with competitive anxiety. This would be to mistake theory for reality and to see anxiety only as a cognitive construct which, because it is always uncomfortable, must be managed away (Corlett, 1996b). Instead, they must attend carefully to how the best coaches and other support staff understand this emotion that always accompanies growth and change. Their work should be aligned more closely with other staff and concern itself more with the major shift in identity that takes place as youth players move towards their dream of becoming first team professionals.

Education, welfare and performance

There have been a number of sport psychology researchers (e.g. Andersen, 2009) arguing about whether there is a clash between encouraging players to attend to performance as opposed to lifestyle and well-being. This argument has extended into a debate surrounding the role of applied sport psychologists and other staff. One side proposes that the role should be to help players with performance enhancement. In opposition to this, some argue that caring for the player is the only legitimate and ethical option for support staff. To some extent this has resulted in a division between those staff whose job descriptions focus on the education and welfare of players and those where there is a clear focus on performance outcomes and results. Our experiences and research suggest that this situation is rarely found in practice at the best football Academies. We will examine this by looking closely at the activities of a number of staff whose identity is fully associated with player welfare. In our work we closely observed the roles of education and welfare staff, sport psychologists and chaplains. Unlike other members of staff, people in these posts are typically perceived to be those who have a major interest in helping players during moments of adversity.

The best clubs have several staff working full-time in the role of education and welfare. Many of these individuals are former schoolteachers. They bring to their role an understanding of the importance of supporting players to acquire a rounded education. They tend to appreciate the demands made on individuals to carry out their educational tasks alongside their responsibilities as players. We saw that best practice involved great attention to the needs of each young person. This area of provision was very much opposed to a one-size-fits-all philosophy. There was a real effort to instil in all players an appreciation of how educational attainment could help them progress in their football and be an important asset for those who fail to achieve professional contracts.

Much of the work involved organising education and training opportunities around the demands of match and football preparation work. This meant that the most effective education and welfare staff possessed high level organisational skills and were skilled communicators. Because of the variability associated with training programmes and match schedules, staff ensured they had close working relationships with coaches and other colleagues in sport science and sports medicine departments. Players and parents were treated on an individual basis, and every effort was made to ensure that individuals committed to their educational programmes. At some clubs this was enhanced through providing schooling on-site. This was the case at Bayern Munich, and it is now commonplace that classroom time is built into the development programme with qualified teachers in support. The advantage to this centres on logistical benefits, flexibility and easing communication between the club and those charged with educating the players. In some clubs there were long-standing relationships between local schools and the Academy. The best were those where staff appreciated the challenges of each other's roles and worked hard to find solutions and compromises where these were necessary. In these clubs we also noticed that there was a shared philosophy about the importance of producing rounded, educated young people. The demands associated with elite level youth football were not allowed to supercede the educational needs of the player. The united front between schools and clubs was highly impressive, and the longevity of the relationships pointed towards a considerable level of mutual understanding. The ultimate sanction of taking the boys out of their football programme tends to keep them focused enough to achieve expected grades.

This open-minded approach to educational provision for young players can be very difficult to achieve for a number of reasons. First, staff at the Academy, including those in education and welfare, are under significant pressure to produce players for the first team. Second, schools who work closely with the football club must be able to demonstrate a track record of success. This means that boys should achieve educational attainment that is appropriate to their ability. That these young people are high level youth footballers is not viewed as an excuse for low achievement. And finally, the head teacher and Academy Director must support each other's vision for developing young players. One senior education and welfare officer explained that the level of personal and professional respect between head teachers and senior Academy staff was the most important factor in guaranteeing the success of this type of work. Because of this, great care was taken to share information and ensure that all decisions that were made were agreed upon and not imposed unilaterally. In some clubs the education and welfare staff had close ties with particular schools because they were former employees or had been pupils there as children. These extra bonds helped provide motivation to smooth the difficult moments between the two organisations.

We spoke to staff and players about the role of chaplains at the club. In an English Premier League context it is rare for a club not to have a chaplain working part-time to support those who need this type of input. These particular individuals are usually highly skilled in providing sensitive pastoral support. This can extend to the young players and may include their families and close friends. The clear focus of the chaplain is on the person rather than the player. The fact that the chaplain could provide a form of help that is unique in a club setting was seen as a great strength. At this point, it is worth noting that chaplains are not involved to aggressively promote a particular religious faith, but are there to offer practical help and a deeper level of spiritual and emotional support where this is needed.

The understanding of education and welfare at a number of top clubs is very sophisticated and subtle. For example, at Middlesbrough, Barcelona, Bolton and Ajax, we were told that all staff contributed to the education of players whether it took place in the classroom, training ground or anywhere else. It was pointed out that the best form of education was through the example of senior players and other staff and that this, rather than more formal and systematic instruction, had the greatest effect. It was explained that this was not only about educating the young person how to become a professional footballer but also about helping the young footballer to become a better person! We reflected on how often we heard this comment across a wide range of clubs, each with different histories and cultures. This was talked about as something that was a clear aim rather than being something that just happened by chance. In relation to this, all Academy staff were constantly reminded that who they were, and how they presented themselves, would have a very important effect on what the players learned. There seemed to be a strong belief that the deepest and most lasting learning often occurs in a non-explicit way. It was quite clear that all Academy staff understood their responsibility to ensure this unconscious learning was associated with positive skills and qualities rather than negative behaviours and attitudes.

And finally, we were struck by how influential Academy Directors were in shaping a rounded and balanced approach to player education and welfare. In our interviews and conversations with these individuals, it emerged clearly that their philosophy had to be something they could articulate to different stakeholders. We were greatly impressed with the depth of knowledge Academy Directors had about the contribution education could make to their players' lives. They also mentioned that they often had to be prepared to make difficult decisions to protect and defend this important part of their work. Most were fully aware that in the first team environment, there were usually significant numbers of staff who were far less supportive about the value of education for young players. Indeed, even at some of the best clubs it was quite common to hear first team staff complain that players must not be overly distracted by pursuit of educational qualifications, and that they wanted them to be more clearly encouraged to focus exclusively on their playing careers. Academy Directors, many of whom had been former professional players, fully understood these first team sentiments. Nevertheless, at the best clubs they skilfully resisted such views and, whether able to convince everyone or not, held firmly to the belief that their professional and ethical responsibility was to provide for the best educational opportunity and playing experience for the young athletes in their care.

Key issues and challenges

A number of important factors emerged from our research into education and welfare provision. In terms of providing support around player welfare, it is equally important that staff maintain the levels of confidentiality seen with sport psychologists. To understand this we need to consider the context within which dialogue between a young player and a member of the Academy staff takes place. There will often be reluctance on the part of the player to talk openly to staff about difficult challenges they are facing. These can range from matters relating to training and match performances, to broader concerns, like those associated with family, coach relationships and peer interaction. There is a natural reservation about talking about these types of matters to people who are involved in player progression and achievement at the club.

At the best Academies, we were told that all staff had a duty to care for the players in their charge, and that it was essential they operated in a consistent and clearly defined way. This helped to build trust and ensured that barriers between staff and players could be reduced as far as possible. The designated education and welfare staff possess experience and specific qualifications that allow them to offer young players a different type of input than the rest of the Academy staff team. We have observed that these individuals spend a great deal of time cultivating a high level of informal communication with the players. The best education and welfare staff had a very good understanding of both the performance demands and lifestyle challenges that the young players typically face. This level of knowledge was essential to ensuring they had credibility with the coaching staff, players and parents. The role required individual members of the staff to be immersed in the day-to-day activities of the Academy to ensure they had a comprehensive picture of all events. However, we noticed that these individuals would also adopt a slightly more withdrawn role to ensure that players understood that education and welfare matters were not directly related to team selection and progress. At some clubs, such as Bolton, Bayern Munich and AJ Auxerre, there were examples of Academy staff emphasising that educational commitment was something all players had to fully embrace. These clubs used a system of punishments to deal with players who did not commit appropriately to their studies. In some cases, this led to players being dropped from teams and even asked to leave the Academy. More usually, these systems were in place to remind players and staff about the importance of education and developing a professional lifestyle.

The best welfare and education staff will have a number of difficult challenges to face because of the holistic perspective they may bring to their work. For example, family conflict and relationship issues at home may mean that a player has to withdraw from training and matches for a period of time. This will need careful, confidential and skilled work. Some of the older players in the Academy may face difficult decisions about going on loan to other clubs. Confidential dialogue with staff could be of great importance in helping them make the best decisions in these situations. We saw that at clubs like Ajax, Bayern Munich and Bolton, loans were not only dealt with by coaching staff but involved a broad number of individuals taking on different responsibilities, including welfare and education staff.

The involvement of parents and close family and friends can be another source of tension and difficulty. Especially for the younger age group, there might be a deep reluctance to speak to the Academy staff about home life and parental ambition. This is a demanding challenge for all young people, especially during the turbulent years of adolescence. With the stakes being so high, and competition for places and achievement being so arduous, it is little surprise that players may feel the best option is to keep things to themselves and work out solutions on their own. We saw how great effort was made to provide structured and unstructured opportunities for dialogue for players and Academy staff. The best clubs ensured that players socialised together with each other and the staff, and that effort was directed at building a close-knit family atmosphere. The preseason programmes seemed carefully designed to achieve this aim, involving a mix of social related activities and performance tasks, to build a team mentality between player and the Academy staff. Rules seemed to have been designed to build respect and ensure negative behaviours like bullying would be kept to a minimum. The best Academies were places where it was very evident that spirit and ethos took precedence over systems and regulations. This was engendered through a series of formal and planned activities, as well as by constant attention to the frequency and quality of personal interaction. The Academy Directors at several clubs, such as Barcelona and Feyenoord, informed us how this strategy reduced the need for more narrow and specific interventions aimed at enhancing players' welfare and well-being. At these same clubs there was a strong conviction that supporting player welfare, education and psychological well-being contributed significantly to player performance in training and matches. There were many critical comments about the view that keeping players well and caring for them as individuals created a less optimal performance environment and undermined players' mental toughness. Indeed, one senior coach at Bayer Leverkusen observed that by taking away any excuses relating to poor treatment of players, their club effectively placed young players in a more challenging learning environment where self-responsibility and developing qualities associated with mentally tough athletes (Cook et al., 2014) was accelerated.

At all of the clubs in our research and applied practice, we came across the concept of development squads. Most usually for players between the ages of 18 and 21, these groups received special attention and support to help them successfully prog-ress to first team and professional environments. A considerable effort was directed at meeting the welfare and well-being needs of these players on an individual basis. Systems of close monitoring and mentoring from coaches, sport psychologists and senior players were commonplace. In around half of the clubs this was done in a systematic and structured way. Other clubs opted to provide this support through more informal channels and in a less systematic fashion. There seemed to be clear recognition that players at this stage needed a different type of support mechanism, one more tailored to individual needs and focussed closely on preparing the young player for the very different culture of first team professional football. Given how close these players were to achieving their goal of becoming full-time professional footballers, much emphasis was placed on guaranteeing confidential and frequent opportunities for dialogues and discussion.

At the best facilities we saw many common features. It was usual to see dedicated classrooms and the latest equipment to ensure a good educational experience. We have seen Academies – for example, at Bayern Munich – where on-site schooling is offered to young players, and teachers and accommodation are in place. Equally, there are examples where carefully worked-out arrangements with high-quality local schools or colleges ensure that an outstanding level of education is available to the players. The advantages to on-site schooling relate to a reduction in logistical difficulties and provide a very visible sign to the players that their football progres-sion and educational achievements are both highly valued. With off-site arrange-ments, the players benefit from a more normal emersion in school life and must make greater efforts to meet the different logistical and scheduling requirements. However, the benefit from being able to experience the typical ordinary life of a young person at school allows them to more easily develop friends and interests beyond their footballing roles.

Conclusion

In summarising this section, we argue that there are a number of very important and common points that we have come across from our applied work and research at some of the best youth development environments in world football. In relation to education, we have seen that the best clubs understand that few young players value this over and above their football-related goals. This reality is the starting point for all of their work in this area. However, from the clubs' perspective, education is not seen as being only about developing academic and vocational skills and knowledge. Instead, it is valued by the best clubs as a way of helping players to understand and take greater responsibility for their own preparation and performances. Staff were con-vinced that it becomes easier to understand and make best use of sport science, sports medicine and psychological information the more educated the player becomes. The best clubs do not undervalue the impact that education and sound welfare procedures can have on player well-being and football performance. They believe that investing in these areas is both ethically correct and will also enhance football performance. These clubs commit extensive financial resources to appoint appropriate staff, provide state-of-the-art facilities and try to overcome all logistical and physical barriers to providing a high-quality educational experience. And finally, education, welfare and well-being are seen as the responsibility of all Academy staff, not just those with more specialist roles, such as chaplains, welfare specialists and teachers.

Based on the research and our applied experiences, we would like to make the following recommendations:

1   Education does not mean only that which is taught formally and in classrooms. The best Academies engender an approach that views the responsibility for education to be everyone's. Education and welfare officers may have the title, but all staff have the role.

2   Players will usually be less motivated towards their academic and/or vocational education in comparison to their football; this shouldn't surprise us. To encourage them to dedicate sufficient effort and time to make a success of this will require the use of rewards and punishments.

3   Psychological well-being can be enhanced through teaching players how to deal with the pressures of competitive performance in football. Staff should help players to develop this knowledge and these skills and understand how they can assist them in their broader lives.

4   Key staff in the Academy and local schools (where these are used) must respect each other's responsibility and roles. The Academy is there to produce first team professional players, the schools and colleges to form educated and/or vocationally trained young people. This tension must be recognised and accepted if it is to provide benefits to the whole person.

5   Investment in infrastructure and equipment to aid education must be matched by recruitment of suitably qualified staff. That means appointing individuals who care deeply about the value of education and who know the culture of professional football.

6   Education should be viewed as something clubs take seriously because of a duty of care. However, beyond the ethical requirement to provide this, clubs should value education because of its links to football performance. Every effort should be made to encourage players and all stakeholders to see that there is a synthesis between education, player well-being *and* performance in training and matches.

7   There are advantages to providing educational provision off-site or on-site; the most important factor in the success of this is the value clubs place on education and how this is conveyed to players, parents and all staff. Clubs must ensure that education is not seen as the easy or soft option, a fallback for those who are not motivated or good enough to achieve as footballers. It must be actively promoted as something that can enhance future lives and current performance in football; an educated footballer can make informed decisions and take more responsibility for his learning. This is key to consistent, long-term, elite level sport performance.

4

COACHING PHILOSOPHY

Who is a coach?

There are literally hundreds of books about coaching in sports and football (e.g. Cook, 2006). Many of these texts will introduce the topic by describing what a coach does, and then begin to refine this to discuss notions of best practice. Especially where the book is aimed at youth sport, there will usually be a section on bad coaching behaviours, only this section will not be called bad behaviour. More likely it will be referred to as inappropriate coaching styles, or ineffective feedback. And especially if this is an academic piece of work drawing on research and theory, the focus will be on behaviour rather than attitudes, beliefs, ethics and morality. There are several reasons for this. First, there is a view that anyone can become whatever they desire, just as long as they are taught the correct skills. Emerging from the psychology of behaviourism early in the 20th century, this perspective has proven to be very appealing because it is totally inclusive. In simple terms, and as its most important advocate, Skinner, argued many years ago, all behaviour is completely shaped by external factors. To get the coaches we need, all we have to do is create the right conditions and reinforce the desired behaviours. Second, there is a dominant zeitgeist, at least in Western societies, that says we have grown past judgemental language such as that which designates some actions as bad or good. Based partly on the psychology of Sigmund Freud, it is argued that we should avoid these terms because they cause feelings of guilt and repressed thinking or, conversely, feelings of superiority and oppressive behaviour. Although rarely acknowledged and even less well understood, this removal of good/bad is also a product of the ideas of existential writers like Jean-Paul Sartre and others, who ushered in the postmodern era and its corresponding belief in relativity. This has been the establishment view for over 60 years now, although on occasion it has been challenged, usually without success. For example, some brave and insightful observers have pointed out that believing in the idea of relativity, that there is no truth and consequently it is impossible to speak of good or bad, is not a relative position in itself. However, these objections have been largely ignored since they appear to be a way to reintroduce a whole body of thinking about ethics and morality that postmodernists would like to see consigned to history.

In the work we have been involved with as practitioners and from research at the world's best academies, it has become very clear to us that despite protestations to the contrary, the most respected, effective and sought-after coaches do not operate as postmodern relativists. They are very clear about what they stand for – what is acceptable and what is unacceptable. The best coaches are guided by their principles, although they often apply these in a flexible way in practice. They also reject the idea that skills are all that is needed to become a great coach. What we have seen and heard is that the best coaches are not defined by their knowledge or skills, but by who they are. It is this quality that the staff at Barcelona, Real Madrid, Ajax, Bayern Munich and others tried to describe in our dialogue with them. When pushed to explain what they meant by this, coaches and other Academy staff spoke about values and mentioned attitudes and beliefs. Some went further and talked about good people, individuals prepared to do the right thing in difficult circumstances, who tried to operate ethically and within a clear moral code (Fairhurst, 2008). This did not sound to us like a description of relativity in action! Although skills and behaviours were mentioned, these were almost always presented as being an extension of the coach's philosophy and identity as a person. This was expressed candidly to us at one club where we were told that coaches who thought they could be effective without possessing an underlying philosophy would eventually be removed from the club. We will examine these important and indeed controversial issues in greater depth in this chapter.

Coaching youth players

Our research participants at all of the clubs we visited in Europe emphasised how important it was that coaches had a passion to work with young players. At Feyenoord, for example, we were told that the coach must be driven in their approach to continuously search out new and better ways to help the young players. They were encouraged to draw any material and ideas from areas outside of football and sport; the accent was firmly on going beyond the familiar. We came across examples where coaches had borrowed and adapted ideas from youth orchestras, drama and dance. Others talked about how important it was to consider new developments in youth work, pedagogy and the training and education of young military recruits. This helped to stimulate new ideas, confirm existing practices and, importantly, keep coaches motivated and excited about their jobs.

Head coaches and Academy Managers were adamant that without this type of motivation the work of the coach would be seriously compromised. At first we were a little surprised by the strength of views expressed about this. Our own experience in the EPL and in a British context was that although coaches might have had considerable interest in working with younger players, most aspired to eventually progress to work in and around first team levels. This was because of greater financial rewards, a desire to coach the best and a desire to enjoy challenges associated with the increased pressure and expectations in a results-focused environment.

In trying to understand this better, it may be useful to consider how this links to the theory of self-determination proposed by Deci and Ryan (1985). Their research revealed that intrinsically motivated individuals tend to persist longer in challenging circumstances and focus more intensely on the task in hand. Coaches with high levels of intrinsic motivation are less likely to assess their competence solely on external measures of success like how close they are to being appointed to the first team. This translates into coaches who are motivated because they are deeply satisfied with their current role. This is because they are doing something for which they have great talent, and have made the choice to coach at youth levels rather than with the first team.

Through this research and our applied experiences, we have also noticed that the more intrinsically motivated coaches tend to be more creative and courageous in their coaching (May, 1975). They seem to be more prepared to embrace change or, somewhat paradoxically, to resist change, especially when it appears to be for no good reason. This is because these coaches are literally in love with their jobs! They hold nothing of themselves back from what they are attempting to do; they are intensely and passionately engaged in the activity of developing young players for the professional game. As Stanley Brard, a very experienced head coach, told us, there are few drawbacks to managing and working with coaches of this type. Humorously, one manager said that the main challenge was to find ways to tell them to go home at the end of the day! There is a serious point here, however, which is that burnout can affect intrinsically and extrinsically motivated individuals equally, especially in high performance, high work ethic based cultures where job insecurity is a constant reality.

We found that at top clubs in Europe, there seems to be a much greater level of respect given to those who decide their vocation is to coach at youth levels. Fewer coaches appeared driven to leave youth and operate in first team environments. It could be said that many of the European staff had a strong personal commitment to coaching young and developing players. Examples of this have been mentioned elsewhere in the book, but it is worth stressing again that at Ajax, Auxerre and Bayern, for example, the Academy coaching team contained a number of very high-profile former players often working with the youngest teams. Some of these individuals had been there for many years; they talked about the need for long-term commitment to become ever more proficient in their roles. This group contained former World Cup players and highly successful ex-professionals. This did not seem to prevent these individuals from being able to work constructively alongside other staff who may not have reached such elevated levels in their playing careers. In this we detected a very healthy disregard for past achievements. The focus was very much on what someone can do to assist the work of the Academy now, and how dedicated they are to this.

At the best clubs, coaches are expected to spend time keeping up to date on recent scientific and coaching literature. The clubs were able to support this through CPD activity and ensuring that staff could take advantage of study leaves and visits abroad, as well as seeing how other sports were coached. There was an opportunity to relate new ideas back to the whole group; coaching and coach education were not seen as separate realities but as different sides of the same coin. A culture of sharing good practice and of challenging each other's coaching approaches was seen as vital to the success of individuals and the group as a whole.

The overriding impression at the best Academies is that coaches are continually adjusting their programmes and input to meet the changing needs of the group of players with whom they are working. For example, at Ajax we were told about how innovations in coaching practice were sought to add value to their programme. Again we encountered the idea that this level of thinking could be sustained only because the foundations and coaching philosophy were well understood and securely held. Coaches were also quick to inform us that good practice was not a matter of delivering a specific and fixed programme over the year for a particular age cohort. The best coaches are sensitive to the fact that each group they work with each year is unique; one set of 15-years-olds can be very different than the same age group in previous years. These differences can sometimes be very substantial. They may be present across all or any of the required physical, technical, tactical and psychological attributes. Although harder to measure, it can also be that the group personality and how it tends to react collectively is unique. And of course across the season, all of these factors at both group and individual levels can change very significantly. Scientific research as well as everyday experience tells us that in any one year of adolescence, huge changes can take place. This demands great flexibility from the coaches in how they manage their programmes and how they work with their players. This type of challenge is much less common in the professional ranks, where most players will be past the turbulent years of adolescent development and have reached greater levels of maturity and stability.

In relation to this, we heard that some clubs held monthly multidisciplinary meetings that focused only on whether the coaching programme needed to change to meet the developmental needs of the players. Decisions were made based on anthropometric and physiological data, observations from other relevant staff and the craft knowledge of the coaches. This final component of the decision-making process has been wrongly described as subjective in some of the coaching and sport science literature. Far more accurate would be to view craft knowledge as the sum total of all the formal and informal learning acquired throughout a career. It is because of the immense scope and breadth of this form of understanding that the best clubs viewed the coach's craft knowledge as being the most important factor in deciding any course of action (Stratton et al., 2004).

We now turn to look at what these coaches are expected to do, how they work with the players on and off the training pitch and the coaching climate they seek to create.

Coaching practice

Nearly every club Academy had a strong ex-player presence in their coaching personnel. They were usually involved in coaching the players 14 and older and were often full-time. They were all fully qualified for the role or working towards the qualifications. This provides continuity and consistency of philosophy, as well as role models the players can interact with. Ajax and Feyenoord were good examples of this with Frank De Boer and Dennis Bergkamp involved with the under-14s and under-15s and Roy Makaay coaching the under-15s at Feyenoord.

Each coach stayed with his group for varying amounts of time ranging from one year to three years. There seems to be an awareness that if coaches stay too long with one group of players there is a danger that decisions can become emotional as opposed to objective. They also had age-range specialists who tended to be coaches who had been employed by the club for many years, were full-time and had gained experience and knowledge in certain age ranges, for example 6–11, 12–14, 15–17 and 18–21.

When we consider coaching methods we often see coaches at the elite clubs using a command style of communication, but their interventions are less frequent than we often see in England. There tends to be more of a variety of coaching methods in England, such as question and answer and guided discovery, which for many helps with long-term learning. Bloom's taxonomy of learning (1956) suggests that after a phase of learning we are all able to gain knowledge or skills or be affected in our emotions or attitude. It is then being able to synthesise and evaluate it to help make better decisions that is the ultimate aim for lifelong learning. To help learners receive information in various ways, more use is being made of visual resources alongside the traditional methods of auditory (e.g. giving instructions) and kinaesthetic (e.g. doing). We have seen the growth of performance analysis and the use of wipe boards and tactics boards as key aids to learning both in the classroom and on the field.

Often we see two coaches working with a squad of players and one will assume the lead role, with the support coach being responsible for the equipment and perhaps warm-ups and cool-downs. However, at Feyenoord they made a particular point that they expected the support coach to also micro-coach so that as the session was being conducted he had the licence to coach individuals without stopping the whole session when appropriate. This obviously needs a lot of trust, communication and understanding between the two coaches. This coaching strategy does provide an opportunity for managing differences and raising self-esteem and confidence, which in turn can fuel motivation and persistence, key attributes of successful people (Kuhn and Jackson, 2008).

All the clubs we have visited and our experiences of best practice suggest that a shared facility with their first team, with sections exclusive for first team use, works most effectively on many levels. Not least this makes the club feel together and builds on that team spirit and camaraderie that is crucial at any football club environment. There is also evidence (e.g. Littlewood, 2005) to suggest that young talent learns from observing older, established athletes and that integrating professionals with youth players' clubs is a great opportunity to facilitate this. Unfortunately, we see many Managers in England who are prepared to compromise this opportunity and even bar their youth players and staff from using the facility whilst the first team are on-site. The subsequent fallout can impact on many levels, including staff relationships, player progressions and recruitment of young players. Perhaps directors and owners need to consider this issue more closely when appointing first team Managers if they really want to foster home-grown talent and minimise the risk on their investment.

The facilities and infrastructure at all the centres we visited were good to outstanding, and conducive to a learning environment. One feature that stands out across our European sample was that all clubs had installed floodlights around most of their pitches. In England this was rarely the case, due to either difficulties with planning permission, lack of commitment to invest or reliance on indoor areas to provide this need. In relation to indoor space, surprisingly, we found that neither Bayern Munich nor Barcelona had an indoor area large enough to accommodate squad training. Werner Kern (Bayern Munich) said it was a conscious decision, as they thought indoor areas were a false environment and could have a detrimental impact on the mentality of the players. He explained that having natural and full-sized areas to train on enhances players' pitch geography and contributes to their overall game craft education.

Coaching what?

Our research and professional experiences point to there being no one fixed way to coach young players. However, this does not mean that there are not some common and universal factors that exist. At a deeper level we believe that the best programmes are able to maintain a dynamic and flexible approach to coaching because they are based on a strongly held, clear vision. This vision may or may not be articulated in documents or club strategy statements; more important is that it can be seen in everything that the coaches do.

There is a strong preference to develop techniques to ensure that players develop feel, touch and balance. This is done in game-like situations as often as possible. It is very clear that the best Academies use small-sided games as the main way to grow skills. In some ways this is similar to the way that actors, surgeons and lawyers are trained. In these professions, all of the necessary technical skills are practiced in vivo as often as possible. That this approach puts individuals under great stress and will often be accompanied by feelings of anxiety (May, 1977) at various points is accepted as an unavoidable challenge (Nesti, 2004). The idea that expert technical performance can be mastered outside of the context for which it is designed is rejected. The best Academies seem to understand that it is not isolated technical skills but in-game technical skills that young players need to learn and master. For example, at Bayern Munich and Bayer Leverkusen, the coaches organised sessions that placed players in stressful situations where techniques and decision making would be developed in a real-world environment. This was also carried out to develop psychological hardiness; this concept has been highlighted by Maddi (2004) as key to performing successfully in highly demanding cultures.

Another key finding from our studies is that the clubs try to provide an environment where play is encouraged. In order to achieve this we have seen coaching teams withdraw into the background once they have set a session off and allow the players to decide how they will carry out the task. This might sound like quite a high-risk procedure. However, as was explained to us, in reality there is little chance that the players will fail. This is because when highly talented and intrinsically motivated young players are placed in 5 v. 5 or similar situations on high-quality, slick playing surfaces and told their task is to play football, a number of things will happen. Naturally, and without the need to intervene, these highly committed young players will play. This means we will see intensity, passion, focus, desire, imagination, creativity and decision making. This is because play is a very serious business, as we can see so vividly when we watch very young children playing. Indeed it could be said that human beings are often more impressive and productive when in a play rather than work mode! Play has unfortunately been given some bad press, especially in those countries imbued with what Max Weber called the protestant work ethic. Research by Csikszentmihalyi (1996) carried out over 40 years across a range of very different performance domains confirms that when a person plays, that is when they focus intently on the activity for its own sake and not on a utilitarian end; they enter the state known as flow. In this experience we become fully absorbed in the task, and a number of incredible paradoxes appear. For example, we are able to forget about time whilst simultaneously being acutely aware of it. Our actions may appear very smooth and effortless, despite the fact that physically and mentally speaking we are operating at our limits. Or again, we can be aware of our surroundings and at the same time not at all self-conscious. There is now a massive body of research in fields as diverse as surgery, warfare, public speaking, dance and sports that highlight the conditions necessary to maximise the appearance of flow (Jackson and Csikszentmihalyi, 1999). This will take place only where the coaches have created a disciplined and focused culture of respect, acceptance of responsibility and joy, rather than one of alienation, disengagement and fear.

This 'less is more' philosophy to encourage player responsibility, intrinsic motivation, the development of courage (Corlett, 1996b) and creativity needs a particular culture. For example, at Barcelona we detected that staff were empowered to manage themselves to a great extent. Formal processes and systems were kept to a minimum. Coaches' own self-evaluation and motivation were seen as the optimum way to create the most dynamic and effective culture. This was enforced by a rigorous recruitment strategy and the rapid removal of coaching staff whose behaviour threatened the integrity of the culture. Such high-trust, high-accountability environments seemed to operate in a way that reduced the need for rigid top-down management, instead providing the opportunity for inspirational leadership (Murray and Mann, 2001) to appear. Some staff recalled how only the most capable coaches appeared able to operate in these types of cultures. They offered examples of poorer coaches who were not sufficiently confident and knowledgeable to succeed in a 'less is more' culture. These were individuals who, often because of a lack of security or misplaced ambition, felt a need to interfere at all times in coaching sessions, and bemoaned the lack of detailed management guidance in the club. As was expressed by Stanley Brard, Academy Manager at Feyenoord, cultures where self-expression are encouraged can work only 'if coaches are self-disciplined, intrinsically motivated and supported. These are not easy places to work in, but they are the best!'

Coaches do not coach young football players only. They coach parents, other coaches and other staff at the club, indeed, everyone who has an important role to play in the life of the player. In this they are arguably the most holistic of staff at a football club. The young player in front of them is a *person*. This term refers to an individual with their own personality, who is always part of and formed by a specific community. The top coach knows this fact, and adjusts his work to meet the player as a person. Some do this because they have strong beliefs based on their own experiences that this is the best way to operate. Other coaches may engage this way due to having read philosophy, psychology (e.g. Maslow, 1968) or other academic literature that explains the concept of person and why this is different than the more fashionable term of *individual*. And yet other coaches may do this because they possess spiritual or religious beliefs that influence how they treat people and what they believe is most important. Whatever the underlying reasons, we have been greatly impressed by the number of youth coaches who insist that they work from a holistic perspective; that is, they try to remember their work is with a whole person and not just a young, promising footballer.

This could be easily seen in the work at Feyenoord and Bayern Munich, especially in the strong system of pastoral support that was in place. This was also formally supported through the education and welfare team. These clubs had made major strides forward in developing closer bonds with the parents and other support networks that were important to the players. This involved much more than formal educational sessions on nutrition, sport science and training programmes. The coaches provided many other informal ways for the players and their parents to get to know one another. Social events, parties, tickets for first team matches and guided tours of the stadium and training facilities, alongside an open door policy, provided opportunities to relate to each other in a more ordinary personal way. The coaching teams were fully behind this approach, despite it requiring some additional commitment. They claimed it contributed to generating a positive collective spirit, helped staff to intervene less harshly and more quickly before things escalated, provided greater knowledge about players' potential and increased the sense of camaraderie and fun for everyone.

One of the new challenges that Academy coaches face in England with the introduction of the new EPPP is to be a facilitator of the complementary sport sciences and to integrate these into the players' individual and squad development programmes. This will require a better understanding of what these functions can provide and how that fits into the bigger picture of the holistic development of the players. The management of this will be vital for the successful graduation of young players into professional careers. There does not seem to be an agreed-upon way to address this work at the best Academies. Some directors and other senior staff suggested that this type of role was better suited to performance directors or football operations staff, leaving coaches to focus more fully on work with players.

In terms of coaching at training and matches, we have already discussed some of the different ways this is carried out at the top clubs. Much of this is informed by current research in football and other sports. The best coaches have the confidence to interpret research and theory and apply this in a creative and dynamic way. Although the academic or research scientist might be reluctant to ignore findings that suggested new ways of working, this is not what we have seen from top youth coaches. Scientific data and theory are compared with existing practice and subject to intense scrutiny. Unless this provides a very convincing case for change, most elite coaches continue with their traditional approaches. This is not because they are conservative or reactionary. On the contrary, most youth coaches we have worked with or observed are constantly thinking about new and better ways of doing their jobs. However, they know the value of the maxim 'if it ain't broke, don't fix it!' And at a deeper level, the best realise that tradition does not necessarily mean merely repetition of the past; it often means continuation of something that works well. After all, a tradition really means a way of behaving or thinking that is based on the sum total of all that has gone before. This must not be denigrated just because it is based on something that is dated, and neither should it be accepted only on the basis that it has been around for a long time. The idea of bringing tradition under the microscope, subjecting it to scientific and non-scientific analysis, seems to be common practice in the world's best Academies.

In Chapter 2, we discussed Ericsson's idea of 10,000 hours of practice to reach elite levels. The somewhat surprising conclusion we have noted is that fewer hours are devoted to this than we might expect from the recommendations of various bodies and researchers. It seems fair to say that there is little evidence that the so-called 10,000-hour rule of talent development is being used to shape practice. If we were to sum up our experiences it would be that the accent is always on quality rather than quantity; top youth coaches appear to be highly sceptical about notions surrounding the optimum amount of time to achieve the best foundations and learning. This is where there seems to very clear agreement.

Much more divergent is the attitude of coaches to the physical preparation and development of their players. This seems to reflect the football philosophy of each club, and how the game is played in the national professional leagues. For example, we found that at Bolton and Bayern Munich there was considerable emphasis on players acquiring physical strength to complement their technical skill in preparation for the first team. This was adjusted depending on the player's position and the physical, anthropometrical and physiological profile of the young footballer. The strongest clubs possess a well-understood vision of what kind of player they hope to produce in this regard. Although there is difference in this area of the coaches' activity, the underlying philosophy is remarkably alike. The best Academies offer their own unique programmes but share a view with other clubs that the coach must keep the requirements of first team football firmly in mind at all times. The aim, as we have said throughout the book, is to develop players for the specific demands of your club. From our experiences and research, it seems fair to say that there is a very strong commitment to this view. The clubs will not be deflected in this task even where this does not satisfy fully the demands that exist at other clubs, or from the various national and international governing bodies of the game (Relvas et al., 2010).

Although there may be quite a diverse way of coaching players on the training ground, we found that these top clubs valued greatly the support of parents in their work, especially with the younger players. All had their own ways of involving parents in their work, but each approached this by ensuring that there was a consistent approach. This was felt to be the most important issue to convert parents' involvement into something useful and positive. For example, at Ajax, Bolton, Middlesbrough and Bayer Leverkusen, we came across a particularly interesting and novel way of involving parents in the work of the Academy. This involved offering parents the opportunity to gain coaching qualifications through club-run classes. Parents were also invited to meet with former Academy players who had progressed to the first team to gain a better insight into the demands and support required. We believe that this type of constructive approach could be adapted and used to great effect in all clubs, irrespective of their size and resources.

There seemed to be an awareness that parents needed to know about what they could do to assist the progress of their sons, but that too much information could be unhelpful or worse. Educating parents about different aspects of player development and the challenges they face as they get closer to the first team was not viewed as a waste of time or a public relations exercise. It was seen as a key method in helping young footballers to become more self-disciplined, focused and able to accept their responsibilities. Formal efforts also took place to encourage an approach that would foster intrinsic motivation and self-determination, the ability to accept failure and challenging situations, and avoid burnout and excessive stress. Parents were routinely invited to meet with coaches to hear how they could enhance this work as key partners.

Lastly, we were told that at the best clubs, considerable efforts were made to communicate important decisions and information to the players and their parents. Carried out through formal and informal methods, most staff we studied and have worked with at top clubs welcomed this type of involvement. This does not mean that coaches abdicated their responsibilities in any way. Coaches kept parents informed but did not seek permission to carry out their work; the strategy was aimed at sharing rather than devolving professional expertise.

The coach as a person

This section will look at who a coach really is in terms of personality, values, skills and attitudes. It is important to remember that a coach is not a teacher; neither are they a mentor, and most certainly not an instructor. Yet coaching shares much common ground with all of these roles and functions. We found that the most effective coaches had a subtle yet very clear understanding of their job – one that usually made some reference to their own philosophy and beliefs about how they should operate (Abraham and Collins, 2011). Technical skills like appropriate use of feedback, active listening, organisation and time management were rarely mentioned. We believe that this was not because these are considered of little importance by expert coaches. After all, the coaches had each been assessed for these skills as part of their coaching qualifications and were subject to continual evaluation by the club. What was striking, though, was the frequency with which we heard reference to the need to make a personal connection with the players. It was pointed out that this did not mean that the coach needed to become a friend to the young player. In fact, some coaches mentioned that being a friend could destroy their educative work and make it very difficult or impossible for learning and development to occur. This point seemed to be at odds with something else we picked up on at most clubs. Coaches were adamant that only those who managed to combine a passion for football and a deep interest in the flourishing of young people would be successful as a coach. And given that such views were so widely and fervently expressed, it seems important to examine these more closely to better understand this.

So what precisely did the coaches mean in talking about their beliefs and philosophy? Skills, as we have said, were mentioned cursorily. Attitudes tended to be addressed more extensively. Coaches spoke about the need to keep an open mind, to be flexible, to avoid looking for easy and quick solutions and to maintain a long-term outlook. They also highlighted the importance of maintaining a strong work ethic, of being patient and respectful of other input from expert and non-expert sources alike. It was possible to detect some small differences between the clubs on these matters. We can speculate that this is due to a number of factors, such as the size of the club, its traditions and its culture. Much of this is very different from the findings from lower level football (e.g. Roderick, 2006; Parker, 1995); coaching practice in these environments tended to be authoritarian, coercive and inflexible.

When the questions surrounding coaching philosophy came up, we found that there was unanimity amongst the coaches that this was the cornerstone of successful development of players. Although each coach articulated their philosophies in different ways and with disparate terminology, it was possible to identify a number of key common themes that emerged. First, at almost every club, coaches talked about the fundamental fact that because most of their young players would fail to progress to the professional ranks at their club, it was imperative that each individual was treated with respect. This was variously described as being about remembering that the young person was entitled to be treated with complete equanimity; all must be treated as equals irrespective of how well they are doing with their football development. Everything should be done to ensure that players not only know this is the coach's philosophy but that they see it in their actions and attitudes consistently and continuously. And the responsibility for this ultimately rests with the individual coaches themselves. It is impossible to assess, evaluate or record this at every moment of the coach's life. This professional philosophy was described by some as being an extension of their deepest held beliefs about what they felt were the most important things in life. At the best clubs there are many coaches who believe that their vocation is about making better human beings, a few of whom will spend some of their lives as professional football players. This idealistic aim, because that is ultimately what this is, can never be fully attained. The idea of an ideal is that it is something worthwhile to aspire to; it does not lose any value or importance just because it is hard to achieve. In relation to this, the best coaches spoke about the need to constantly remind themselves of this ideal, their basic philosophy of professional practice and the effort required to keep this alive despite the demanding and competitive environment they existed in.

The beliefs that coaches had about who they were, their roles and their responsibilities were also very connected to their own formative years as young players in the game. Most influential seemed to be how they had been affected positively by inspirational coaches during their earliest introduction to the game. It seemed that as their first teachers, these coaches had created deep and long-lasting impressions. Most mentioned that they had encountered special people who happened to be football coaches. These individuals had a particular philosophy, one that seemed very similar, even where they differed considerably in terms of personality. This philosophy seemed once again to be grounded in ideas about people rather than the sport.

It is this that we heard much about throughout the research and our work in the game. Inspirational coaching is about inspirational people – those who see their role in terms of vocation. The idea that was most frequently spoken about at the clubs was that players learn most through encountering coaches who direct their passion, knowledge and skills through the synthesis of the personality in such a way that all learning feels like a personal encounter – one where the individual player believes and feels that his growth and progress is as important to the coach as it is to him. This rare but key quality is the reason that a young player will develop unshakeable trust in the coach. And this level of trust will in turn allow the individual to take responsibility for his own learning and achievements (Chelladurai and Trail, 2006). It is this vital but very tangible factor, rather than good feelings or reassurances, which is the most important benefit of being formed by inspirational coaches.

Based on the research and our applied experience, we would make the following recommendations:

1   Coaches should possess a coaching philosophy that is based on a synthesis of their own experience, scientific research and theory. This will enable them to practice their art consistently and creatively.
2   Clubs should create a climate where coaches see their role as a vocation working with young people. This means that intrinsically motivated behaviour should be encouraged, and coaching should be seen as a personal task.
3   Academy coaching should involve many experiences of flow – for the coaches and players alike. The conditions – individual, organisational and cultural – that

make flow states more likely to occur are well understood and must be put in place by the clubs.

4   When it comes to coaching interventions on the training ground and in matches, the mantra should be 'Less is more!'

5   Parents must be involved in the coaching process in a way that is clear, consistent and useful. Parents are not a problem, and neither are they the solution – rather, they are potential that can make an important contribution to their son's progress.

6   Coaching off the field of play will often be more important than on. Coaches must see their job holistically – everything counts.

7   The numbers of hours acquired at the training ground, in matches or in the gym is much less important than the type of experience gained. The mantra should be 'Quality, not quantity!'

5

SPORT SCIENCE PHILOSOPHY

Introduction

Sport science as an academic discipline in the UK emerged in 1975 at Liverpool John Moores University. The first cohort of students on the new BSc (Hons) in sport science studied psychology, physiology and biomechanics. Unlike many other multidisciplinary sport science degrees that would be developed in the years that followed, this course included a strong focus on football. This reflected staff interests, especially individuals like Professor Tom Reilly. A passionate supporter of Everton Football Club, he became the first person in the country to complete a PhD in physiological factors, ergonomics and training within high level professional football. Since that time, interest in the study of sport science and football has expanded dramatically. Universities, research centres, sports governing bodies and professional football clubs have all contributed to this growth throughout the world. This has resulted in more academic research and applied interest into how sport science can enhance performance in the game, and especially at the highest levels.

It was only a matter of time before this greater level of knowledge about sport science began to filter down to youth levels, particularly at the top football clubs. These organisations possessed the resources to bring sport scientists in to help shape work in areas like fitness, strength training and performance analysis. Clubs were keen to see their young players become more educated about the optimum way to prepare and train, and sport science was viewed as an important part of this strategy. Owners and CEOs started to demand better returns on the money invested in the development of young players. A scientific approach, where evidence could be used to guide actions and justify decisions, became a common and normal feature of first team operations and in elite youth Academies. This expansion in knowledge and greater acceptance of the benefits of sport science also impacted on the practice of coaches. They were required to study the different sport science disciplines as part of coach education courses and coaching awards, and to demonstrate an under-standing of how this new information could be applied in their work with players. Sports scientists were recruited to join clubs on a full-time basis, and few outside of the top levels in England at least were without two or three of these individuals. Within the youth sections and Academy level, staff were keen to emulate the devel-opments that had taken place at first team levels. There was a real drive to employ more sports scientists in full-time roles or as part-time consultants, to assist the work of the coaches and accelerate the progression of players to the professional ranks.

Our research and experience suggest that despite this initial enthusiasm to greatly increase the numbers of sports scientists working in youth football, this did not occur everywhere, including at some of the best clubs in the world. We think this is because of a number of interrelated factors, which we intend to discuss in this chapter. Some of these are due to misunderstandings, lack of finance and frustration over difficulties around integrating science into football. Others are wider rang-ing and arguably reflect the challenging environment and culture of professional and high level football. Although it may at first glance appear that this has been an unfortunate state of affairs, it will be argued here that this is not necessarily the case. We will suggest that the failings, challenges and missed opportunities point towards the need for a radical rethink about the role and involvement of sport science in youth football.

Evidence from the research and our experiences convinces us that understanding about what does and doesn't work in relation to the application of sport science in youth football is at an advanced stage. In the clubs in particular, there are signs of a recognition that we are at a moment where no further significant improvements will occur without a major rethink about how football should integrate science into its practice. In some ways this chapter may appear to contain a mixed message, or at least one that may seem rather ambiguous. After advocating that football should embrace science more fully, it might appear that we are arguing that this has gone too far in some ways. We hope that what follows will make it apparent that there are new and more productive ways of looking at the area of sport science support in football at youth levels – approaches that ensure science is in the service of football rather than the other way around!

Sport science provision

Our pan-European research revealed that contrary to what might be expected, very few of these elite clubs employed more than one or two full-time sports scientists on their staff. For example, at Bayer Leverkusen we found only two full-time staff working in sport science related roles. This was quite a surprise given the extensive involvement of these types of individuals in first team environments, and because of the very considerable growth in the numbers of newly qualified graduates with sport science related degrees at both undergraduate and postgraduate levels. Most of the European clubs in the study, and the majority we have observed or worked at in England, have relied on part-time staff or university students on placements or internships to help with fitness testing, designing strength and conditioning programmes or advising on nutrition. The only area of sport science that has seen a rapid increase in numbers of full-time staff has been that of performance analysis. These individuals who have acquired considerable knowledge and expertise in performance analytics have become more familiar in many youth sections and Academies. Often utilising tools like Prozone, they have revolutionised the amount of up-to-date match and training data that coaches (and players) can access. However, as our research data shows, this is very different from other areas of sport science, where only two clubs out of the eight studied had more than one full-time member of staff working in this area.

The view expressed at the clubs we visited about sport science was that this might be the next essential area to develop because it had not fulfilled the early promise that was attached to it. At Bayer Leverkusen the head of the Academy mentioned that they tended to use some of the other sports coaches from their sports club to develop specific areas such as explosive speed. When discussions turned to the sport science discipline of sport psychology, staff were almost unanimous in pointing out how little had been done to address this properly in their clubs. This was in spite of it being frequently identified as the most important factor in successful transition to the professional ranks and first team levels (Brown and Potrac, 2009). Jan Olde Riekerink, Academy Manager at Ajax, suggested that the psychological elements of a player's make-up were the most important: "You can have little talent and a great attitude but if you have a lot of talent with a poor attitude the chances are you will not succeed at the highest level."

From our own experience and the research, it is clear that only very rarely has this key area been attended to in any systematic and organised way. Given the emphasis staff placed upon this, whilst at the same time acknowledging its surprising absence, we feel that a closer scrutiny is required to understand such a paradoxical situation. The study data and our own applied experience in clubs over many years confirmed that most clubs rarely employed more than part-time input from sport psychologists, and that much of this was carried out by academic staff from local universities. Given its importance, we will examine this situation more closely in Chapter 7 and identify new ways to bring the benefits of sport psychology closer to the clubs. It will become clear that there are very real obstacles to the acceptance of sport psychology in the clubs at this level, and that it will need a change from the clubs and sport psychologists to be able to carry out effective work in the future.

More promisingly, elite level Academies have been using sports scientists for a number of years to help gather data on fitness related work, to design and oversee preseason training programmes and to provide up-to-date information on physical factors that coaches can use to monitor team and individual performances. The biggest change in recent years has been the involvement of sports scientists in helping coaches to adjust training loads to maximise physiological fitness during coaching sessions on the training ground over the week. This detailed information emanating from the sports scientists and their equipment has been welcomed generally by the coaches. It has been seen as another vital tool in the task of preparing players optimally. The specific benefits from this activity are usually seen in at least three crucial areas: injury prevention, game preparation and recovery from fatigue. Most of the coaches we have worked with or spoken to during our research were always very positive about the benefits of including sport science data to guide their practices. Some of this could be because of the increased understanding that coaches have about sport science and the improvements it can have on applied practice. But there are likely other reasons behind this increased openness to new ideas and information. For a number of years now there has been a movement in many areas of society, for example in business, education and health, where all decisions and actions are expected to be based on solid objective data. We live in an era when everything has to be justified in terms of evidence-based practice. No longer are individuals allowed to hide behind explanations for their actions based on statements such as 'we have always done it this way!' Past behaviours and traditions are seen as acceptable or good only if they can be defended scientifically. This is seen as the way to avoid bias, subjective decision making or doing something merely from habit.

The result of this philosophy should mean that the role of the sports scientist should expand and grow. Assisted by ever more rigorous measurement technologies, their impact upon youth football at elite levels could be expected to increase dramatically. In the future we might see that sports scientists will become more numerous in the clubs and begin to exert much more influence on all aspects of performance. Maybe clubs will even get to the situation where coaches are outnumbered by sports scientists because they can provide the hard data to support their activities and advice, something that coaches are unable to do. CEOs and owners with huge financial investments in teams and their Academies may feel more reassured by the scientifically robust decisions of their sport science staff in comparison to the more *ad hoc*, less systematic and difficult-to-quantify input of the coaches.

And yet, our research findings from several elite football Academies across Europe and our own engagement in a number of English Premier League clubs reveal that rather than an increase in sports scientists, numbers have remained quite low, and involvement continues to be relatively small. In some branches of sport science, like nutrition, this is very evident. If nutrition and diet are as important as the science claims, why do so few clubs have full-time staff providing this type of support? We didn't find any clubs who employed a full-time nutritionist but found several, such as AJ Auxerre, that sought nutritional advice from specialists. One would have thought that the argument is even stronger in an Academy setting given the importance of correct diet and healthy eating for youth athletes in particular (Bishop, 2010). There is a large body of scientific research that supports this, albeit that very few studies have actually been carried out in football at elite levels (Williams, 2013). The same is true about the importance of ensuring that teams and individual players follow fitness programmes based on sound scientific research. Again, studies abound, including some in football (Svensson and Drust, 2005). These confirm that specific practices and interventions should be followed to optimise player conditioning and physical fitness.

Based on the research and our experience inside clubs in various roles, we believe that there are very real reasons why sports scientists and sport science have not had the involvement and effect that could reasonably be anticipated given the very considerable advances in research and knowledge in the area over the years. We will turn to this now, but before we do it is worth pointing out that no one party, it seems to us, is the main culprit in causing this state of affairs; all have been guilty of some amount of intransigence and failure to appreciate the others' points of view. Rather than blaming either side, it is our belief that the major problem has been one of philosophy rather than science. The importance of constructing a philosophy of science that could enhance the use of sport science knowledge in youth football is something we will now explore in more detail.

Whither sport science?

Youth Directors and Coaching staff appear convinced that the knowledge brought by ever more sophisticated sport science understanding has great potential to improve the progression of young players to first team levels, and the EPPP is providing a framework from which data can be interrogated and inform this holistic development. We have encountered across European clubs and in the English Premier League many senior staff who point out that sport science is not the problem. The difficulty is more about how the data is converted into useable information, and the way it is conveyed to coaches. To begin to understand these two issues more fully, it is worthwhile to look a little closer at the culture of youth sections and Academies, and the pressures faced by the staff in carrying out their work.

As we have already seen, the culture at some of the best Academies in the world could be described as involving a blend of science and art. There is great attention to detail. This can be seen through the efforts to subject so much of what goes on to some form of measurement, assessment and evaluation. At Feyenoord we came across a good example of this activity in their protocols for development. The biggest sport science influence on the whole Academy is the Raymond Verheijen Football Fitness Periodisation Model. This model underpins all their physical programmes, and they have seen the benefits, with the players looking fresh in the second half of the season, getting better fitness scores on the tests and fewer soft tissue injuries, and the players who are making the transition to the first team looking as fit or fitter than those established in the group. As the Academy Manager explained to us, every effort is made to gather as much useful scientific information on the players as is feasible, to guide training and inform decisions on player retention. On the other hand, there is a deep awareness that it is not really about these things, and that, ultimately, the success or failure of all concerned is based on the production (an unfortunate word, but a reality nevertheless) of players for the first team. And the more experienced and knowledgeable the coach or other members of staff are, the more they know that this *feels* more like an art form than a purely scientific enterprise. Immediately, therefore, this different philosophy about development and learning can bring a potential source of misunderstanding and tension into the relationship between some sports scientists and coaches. This is because, as scientists, most sports scientists have been trained to see measurement as the best way to assess learning, change and development. The position could be expressed somewhat crudely by the idea that if something can't be measured then it is impossible to know it exists. Ironically, this position is based on the views of various materialist and positivists such as the philosopher, Wittgenstein, who famously said that 'what we cannot measure, we should not speak about'! This is clearly a problematic world view when our attention turns to ideas like courage, humility and other more psychologically based concepts. It is also not easy to apply to ideas in the biological sciences either on occasions. For example, sport scientists have pointed out to coaches that concepts like VO2 max and the anaerobic threshold do not actually exist. These and many other sport science constructs cannot be exactly and precisely identified as one could with physical phenomena like magnetism. Therefore, where the sports scientist has been educated and trained to approach their work in this positivist way, there will likely be much potential for disagreement with non-scientists and other staff who view science quite differently.

This alternative way of seeing things could prevent much misunderstanding and conflict between sports scientists and coaches. We need only think about how coaches are sometimes written about in popular literature. The best coaches have often been described in language closer to philosophy, literature or even poetry than in more scientific terms. For example, outstanding coaches have been lauded as inspirational mavericks, charismatic personalities or intuitive decision makers. Rarely are they held up as rigorous scientists, masters of measurement or systematisers of data. Indeed, at a number of clubs, including Feyenoord and during our time working at Bolton with Sam Allardyce and Mike Forde, great efforts were made to facilitate understanding and better communication between coaches and scientists. In the case of Bolton, this involved holding a large number of staff away days over the season. At these events, attended by all full-time staff, attempts were made to resolve conflict, disagreement and misunderstanding across a range of operational and strategic issues, including the effective application of science in football. These away days were organised at first team, Academy and whole club levels to help staff to understand their part in the big picture, gain common practice and build inter-disciplinary relationships.

Given the very different educational experiences and guiding philosophies of many sports scientists and coaches, it should not be a surprise that disagreements and misunderstanding are commonplace. We have spoken to coaches and sports scientists about their roles and the frustrations they have in relation to each other's activities. The level of knowledge that coaches have about sport science at many top clubs is extremely advanced. Although our view is that sports scientists have significantly less understanding about best coaching practice in comparison to that possessed by most coaches at this level, they nevertheless usually have a good grasp of what makes an excellent football coach, and the different types of skills and abilities needed to work effectively with young players. For their part we found the coaches to have a sound appreciation of some key scientific principles relevant to football.

For example, coaches at elite clubs were able to discuss the importance of periodisation in preparing players optimally at different phases of the season. Although they may have lacked some underpinning scientific knowledge about how, for example, specific muscles react at the molecular level during a set training programme, there was good awareness about the basic physiological principles behind their work. Most sports scientists were prepared to accept that the coaches had acquired impressive levels of knowledge about the science of training, and that rarely was a lack of this type of understanding a major obstacle in their work together. At many clubs we were told that coaches had gained additional qualifications in physical education or sport science and had to continually improve their scientific knowledge and understanding by attending specific training programmes and academic conferences on football and sport science. Although we frequently heard complaints that these events tended to be too academically orientated and based on research lacking in ecological validity, there was a general consensus that it helped coaches think more carefully about their own practice and better ways to incorporate scientific findings in their work.

However, this is not to say that there are still not very fundamental problems between coaches and sports scientists. Our findings and experiences in the game highlight that without a new way of working, one that is based on a different type of philosophy, sport science and sports scientists will see their role and involvement diminish even further at the best clubs. This may sound rather an alarmist perspective to adopt, and one that is not really supported by the current situation. However, our research allowed coaches and sport science staff to provide in-depth accounts over a period of time. As we discussed in the introduction, the methodology behind the study enabled us to capture data that would have been difficult to access with another approach. A crucial aspect of the study was that we were able to build up trust because of the longer-term engagement we had with key individuals. This allowed us to guarantee that all information gathered through formal and informal means would be completely confidential, and anonymity would be assured. It is due to this approach that the staff in these world-class Academies were prepared to speak freely and offer, at times, very candid opinions.

One of these findings was that it became increasingly clear that staff were aware that important changes were necessary to ensure sport science could have an increased impact. They described their concerns about how the general view seemed to be that the solution being offered focused largely on recruitment of more sports scientists into clubs. This seemed to be a poorly thought through position according to many we've spoken to because in their view a fresh and new approach was urgently required. There was considerable frustration that sport science in the Academies seemed intent on following models in the first team and that the answer seemed to be about more of the same instead of developing their own alternative approach.

It is possible to view this from a broader perspective about innovating and managing change. One way to look at this suggests that there is too much consensus; it all appears very comfortable and reassuring. The generally accepted view is that increased levels of sport science support in youth football will bring corresponding benefits. In this climate, dissenting voices tend to be easily dismissed as belonging to frightened traditionalists, reactionaries or those who can't understand the new orthodoxy.

A challenge to this is that it is precisely at these moments, where everyone is apparently united in one view, that real and deep change is most needed and usually about to take place. We believe that this is the stage we are facing right now. Inside the very best clubs there is a sense of discontent. For example, several senior staff at AJ Auxerre told us about their reservations concerning how newly qualified sports scientists in particular often seemed incapable of appreciating that there are limits to what science can tell us. Referred to as *scientism,* this mind-set believes that it is only through use of the scientific method that we can have confidence in anything we say or do. This type of unthinking and arrogant position has been subject to power-ful critique (Fforde, 2009). It has been argued that scientism is often found in poorly educated scientists and those who behave like technicians than in those with a more in-depth and advanced level of knowledge. Even within the academic community itself it has been claimed (Nesti, 2004) that the narrow and limited education of some sports scientists is the major obstacle to its wider acceptance, rather than it being the result of a rejection of science *per se*. To conclude, it seems fair to say that based on our research there remains great enthusiasm for using scientific ideas and principles to improve practice in the clubs. On the other hand, the view seems to be that sport science in football has promised much but failed to deliver fully to its potential. A new approach is needed, and especially one suited to the reality of working with young players in Academy settings.

The art of coaching science

The complaint we have heard time and again is that sport science could be so much more effective and useful if it was not delivered by sport scientists! Let us explain. Coaches are keen to incorporate the best that science can offer into their coach-ing work. However, this must be done in a way that respects the very particular demands of the game. This refers not only to the physical, technical and tactical aspects of football but also to values, to the environment, and to the culture within which the activity must take place. So it becomes a very important issue to identify what this culture is and why it is so important to adapt and meet its demands. Quite simply, it is a culture that we would argue has more in keeping with that found in the arts than in the laboratory or the scientific research centre. This may come across as a rather fanciful suggestion. Surely at an elite club, even at youth level, there is a precise focus, an intense dedication to develop and select the best. In some ways it might seem much more reasonable to argue that Academies have more in common with military training camps where young recruits are inculcated into a specific culture, trained systematically and selected or rejected. We do not think this is what happens in the best football clubs. Whilst it is true that self-discipline, mental toughness, teamwork and organisation feature strongly, football clubs are preparing boys to play football, not to survive mortal combat. And the word *play*, as we discuss in the chapter looking at sport psychology, is a hugely important conceptual term in this sport and most definitely at the highest levels and not only for youth footballers.

We believe that from what we have seen and heard, many elite level Academy and youth coaches see their role as being more about forming people who will become successful footballers, rather than creating great athletes who will be able to perform the tasks associated with achieving in football. This means that sport science must be made to fit the person in the same way that that technical and tactical needs are, and not the person to fit the science. In practical terms this may mean that often scientific principles will be applied creatively. We saw this at Feyenoord, Ajax and Bayer Leverkusen, where staff used a number of different ways to integrate science into the activities of the players. One example involved using a mentoring scheme involving older players working with younger groups on an individual basis to help them apply nutritional advice and flexibility training into their broader lifestyles. The best coaches we have worked with and met during our research are deeply aware that science is not and can never be a static concept. They know that it is dynamic and continually evolving to meet new challenges and contexts. There is awareness that it can never be the last word because science is really only about method, and methods are about how something is done. They are not concerned with the more important and fundamental questions about what should be done and why. This is the domain of philosophy – not the academic subject, but the questions behind the deeper meaning that governs choices and actions. This means that for the best coaches, the application of sport science knowledge in football is a personal enterprise. The coach or sports scientist will need to draw on all of their experiences, feelings and beliefs when wrestling with understanding some scientific data, or where they are faced with utilising some scientific information to improve specific tasks. However, this type of activity should not be called subjective! This term refers more precisely to decision making that is based solely on feelings and emotion.

Training, especially of the physical sort, must always proceed from the reality of the game and the culture of the sport. All science and any type of intervention must be grounded in the reality of the game at elite youth levels. It should always be tested against its capacity to impact the sport as it is played in real life, not as it is modelled or discussed in the abstract terms of theories. This is not an anti-science stance. Instead, this perspective advocates that scientific knowledge should be used in a way that is aware of its potential benefits and strengths, but that is always cognisant of its limitations and weaknesses. Science has complete competence in matters related exclusively to science. In reality, very few such situations exist, and clearly in human enterprises, science must be used to serve human needs and not to control, reorder or subvert these.

In light of this we are convinced from our research and applied experiences that the most outstanding coaches (and sports scientists) at elite level youth football are expert philosophers of science. As Stanley Brard put it at Feyenoord when talking about the application of science, "Having a philosophy about what is useful and when it can be used is a highly practical tool, not just a comforting idea that can help you avoid the necessity to choose and make decisions!" Coaches of this sort constantly keep in mind the distinction between means and ends. This is about understanding the important distinction between how and why something is done. The why, that is the ultimate purpose and goal, must always take precedence over the how, that is the methods and processes. Unfortunately, this is not always seen in practice. In football and across society, some commentators have warned that we are becoming 'consumed by process' and forgetting or ignoring the vision aimed for (Csikszentmihalyi, 1996).

In the best environments we have seen coaches and sports scientists who constantly keep the desired end in mind at all times. In their approach they seem to be following the ideas of the greatest philosophers of the ancient world such as Socrates and Aristotle, although maybe few of them have ever read any of the works of these thinkers. These individuals argued that "it is the philosophy in which one believes, not the technique, that must govern one's life and come first" (Corlett, 1996a, p. 88). This means that these coaches and scientists constantly shape the information they accrue from their sport science technologies and methods to fit the needs of their players. They do not rely on scientific data to drive their decisions. Instead they use it to challenge their own perceptions and confirm practices that have been developed to meet the situations they face. And there is a deep awareness that no two circumstances are ever the same; the only constant is change and newness. This does not mean that there are no underlying fundamental principles that always exist and therefore must be acknowledged by the coach or sports scientist. It does mean, however, that there is a requirement for scientific facts to be turned into living ideas if they are to effect change in the way intended. And in applying these facts the desired end must be kept in mind at all times. Sport science in football is not about producing impressive figures and elegant models; it is about helping players improve, recover and get better.

Education and training

The training and education of those who apply sport science in Academies should be much like that of the first team staff. They will need to have a good grasp of theory, research and new thinking in the area. This is most effectively acquired through a combination of formal study and through practice. The best coaches and sport science staff we have encountered talked about the importance of keeping their knowledge up to date and being careful not to rely on what they had previously learnt. We came across this perspective at many clubs and very clearly at Feyenoord and Ajax. They stressed the need to reflect on the importance of the scientific information they had access to, and to think deeply about how they had applied this and how useful it had been in improving their work. In describing this, some staff pointed out that this way of being able to analyse and engage in critical thinking was like part of the DNA of the highest achieving individuals. At some clubs we were told about people being removed from posts or failing to secure jobs because of their inability or refusal to think in this way. From our discussions about this it became clear that this was viewed as one of the key attributes of a professional person. A professional was described as someone who, despite having considerable relevant knowledge and understanding of the task, is always seeking new and better ways to operate. This might mean they develop new skills, adapt old ideas or generate completely new approaches. The important quality here is that they take responsibility for this. In the words of Rollo May (1977),

> the person who has the courage to create; they are prepared to take a step away from the safe and secure path of how things have always been done, to a new and unfamiliar place that could bring either success or failure.
>
> (p. 56)

Although not easy to identify with a precise definition, our impression has been that the more educated the individual is, the more prepared they are to engage in the thought processes and actions we have just described. Education here does not refer to formal qualifications, although it does not of course preclude these. Rather, it means that the educated coach or sports scientist is someone who knows their area well enough to know how much they do not know! It also refers to a capacity to be able to think broadly or narrowly as the situation demands. And finally, it describes the person themselves. An educated person should ideally be one who is open to new ideas but prepared to accept them only after careful, sustained and in-depth scrutiny. In contrast, coaches in particular made highly critical comments about the ineffectiveness of people they had worked with who had been trained well but lacked education. The distinction being made here seemed to be that the trained individual often relies on the application of techniques and behaves as though the data can answer the question on its own. This is in contrast to an educated and trained approach, where data is converted into information and then applied to the task, and technical skills are used to gather and collate data and not to provide the solution.

The demands placed on Academy staff also include another key issue that appears sometimes to have been overlooked in the professional game. The majority of sport science research has been carried out with sub-elite, adult, amateur sports performers. Great care therefore needs to be exercised in interpreting the findings from these studies into an environment with elite youth footballers, some of whom within the older age groups could be considered as full-time players. Given the lack of a large body of sport science research with this group, it is even more important that coaches and sports scientists take great care to interpret the existing knowledge in sport science. Sometimes this will result in new approaches and adaptations. On other occasions it will mean that the science and associated research findings are rejected.

In some ways it could be argued that this is consistent with what Maslow (1968) said about the need to humanise science and psychology to ensure it serves its real purpose. He pointed out that if science does not fit the person, so much the worse for science. In these circumstances the answer is to change the science, not to change the person! The responsibility for this rests with each individual member of the staff. They cannot avoid or evade the responsibility to think creatively and take action to ensure that science serves, not controls. This will require understanding, skill and courage. However, in the best Academies it was very evident that there is also the broader issue of culture to consider. Staff will be confident of acting in this professional manner, that is of applying science creatively and in a contextually appropriate way, only in cultures where this type of behaviour is supported and encouraged.

Culture, values and sport science

We have been fortunate to have worked inside some clubs where a culture exists that is conducive to maximising sport science support. The clubs with some of the best Academies in the world have also grown these types of cultures, deliberately and over time. In these places there are a number of common features, which relate to staffing, leadership and values. These can be found across national boundaries and are not constrained by size of the club, resources or wealth. For example, at Feyenoord we found that there was a clear aim to create a culture where the input from sport science staff would be welcomed even when this challenged existing practice or orthodoxies. This was memorably described by the head youth coach at one of the most successful clubs in the world as being about "creating a comfortable culture in order to nurture uncomfortable thinking!"

In these environments, great care is taken to recruit staff with a deep passion for their area of expertise. In Academy football this would mean taking on individuals who have a vocation to work with young people who are striving to become professional footballers. They would also be expected to have extensive knowledge about sport science and how this can be used in football to develop more and better professional players for the club. This may not sound like a radical demand on behalf of the club. On the contrary, we believe that this is a huge challenge facing all clubs, in that it emphasises that it is not the academic knowledge of the sports scientist that is most important, but their commitment to producing players for the first team. By building up a team of such people, a very particular type of culture will eventually emerge. This will be a place where every decision and suggestion is scrutinised to see if it can help support the development of young players. Everything, from the value of specific types of data to measurement protocols to how information is conveyed, will be analysed, discussed and argued about. Nothing will ever be able to slip through the net to reach the players, unless and until it has been looked at from every conceivable angle. And if some idea or intervention does not survive this intense investigation, it will be amended or dismissed. This will be a culture unafraid to say no. Indeed, in our experience and study of the best, it will be a culture where many things will remain constant, or at least appear so, because there is so much effort being directed at thinking about what could be changed!

To facilitate this there will need to be sustained and constant encouragement for staff to think creatively, suggest innovation and take risks. This type of activity will be applauded, rewarded and expected. That it very often does not result in clear, immediate or substantial alterations to practice is a frustration that must be accepted. Humility, selflessness, and a willingness to share opinions, take criticism and pursue difficult paths are all essential in this culture. Leaders are vital to nourish this form of culture, and in Jim Collins' book *Good to Great* (2001), he identified these as Level 5 Leadership qualities. This means that the senior staff and managers will back their sport science and coaching staff as they adhere to these types of roles. The leaders will not assess their staff so much on what action they can visibly see, or on how busy they are, but instead on the knowledge, passion and focus they bring to the task. And that task ultimately is about doing everything that can be done to bring players into the first team professional ranks at the club. This view was endorsed at several clubs, including Ajax, where Jan Olde Riekerink emphasised that they have a coaching plan that is based around developing the right mental attitude, which he demonstrated by showing a couple of clips of a before and after of a player who wasn't closing down quickly enough or with a determined attitude.

The final word is about ethics and morality. The optimum cultures we have seen where sport science can flourish best and fulfil its valuable role are where there is serious conviction about the medical maxim, derived from the Hippocratic Oath: the main concern is to do no harm. Staff need to know that this is formally and informally enshrined in the culture. The leaders at the club and the Academy must support this through their own behaviour and ethos. Ultimately, bad ethics and amoral decision making will negatively affect success, at least in the longer term. In the shorter term it may seem that the damage can be managed; this is an illusion because poor ethics destroy trust, and this quality of a culture is the basis of all they do. Trust in the sport science interventions, innovation and changes to practice is less based on the validity of the science. It is always more about trust in the person, their values and their moral compass. At the very best Academies, this is engendered through building a collective ethos and spirit, and by supporting sports scientists and coaches who possess the integrity to reject good ideas with bad ethics in favour of better ideas with sound ethics. If this sounds too idealistic and unattainable, maybe the following words from the former Head of the Academy at Bayern Munich, Werner Kern, will convince you: "we are responsible for the boys and their holistic development. That means we plan diligently with qualified staff to maximise potential."

Based on the research and our applied experiences, we would make the following recommendations:

1   Sport science theory and research findings must always be interpreted and adapted to fit the needs of young footballers and the demands of high level Academy football.
2   Coaches and sports scientists should subscribe to a shared philosophy of science – one where the laws of science are always secondary to the reality of human beings.

3   The growth of sport science in Academy football should be through increased numbers of coach–scientists rather than appointing more sport science staff.

4   The application of sport science knowledge in Academy football is an art form; it is a personal enterprise and needs a personalised approach.

5   It is vital to guard against collecting more and more scientific data just because the technology exists; meaning should always override measurement!

6   Clubs should avoid recruiting sport science staff who possess technical skills but lack a broad scientific education.

7   Clubs should create a culture where science is supported, sustained, subjected to critical analysis and continually examined in relation to ethics and morality.

6

COACHING PRACTICE AND SPORT SCIENCE SUPPORT ON THE GROUND

In this section we are looking at areas of development that we have witnessed or employed ourselves in our various roles within professional football. This is not meant to be an in-depth investigation into all aspects of development, as this is beyond the scope of this book; however, we will touch on areas we feel are the most important in terms of actual practice (rather than theory or policy) on the ground at the clubs visited and known to us.

The activities of the staff should be driven by the clubs' vision and philosophy regarding what type of players they need to develop and what they need to do to achieve that. In terms of some of the most successful clubs in Europe, this was plain to see. If we think about the types of players being produced at Manchester United, Ajax and Barcelona, we can see they fit a style and type that is commensurate with their playing philosophy. Manchester United and Ajax have always produced wingers who can dribble past defenders, whereas we see more multifunctional-type midfield players at Barcelona to fit their short passing game. All the clubs we have visited had a possession-based philosophy encouraging their players to take responsibility with and without the ball, and this was reflected in their training and match-day practices.

Reilly and colleagues (2000) observe "Talent development requires an environment conducive to learning and an on-going process of talent identification and selection." Although we have not discovered any blueprints that guarantee success, there are common themes we can explore that minimise the risk of failure.

It must be remembered that children develop at different rates in different domains. They are moving targets that are often unpredictable and resource hungry. We often see that early physical development is not matched by their technical and tactical understanding, which can be neglected for short-term gains that often result in long-term disappointment. We see an array of learning curves from the negative curve, whereby quick early gains then taper off and plateau, to the S curve, where we see initial improvement followed by a dip and then another improvement. Of course coaches and staff want to see more of a linear improvement, but this very rarely happens in development football.

Once the talent has been identified and the players recruited, what do some of the best clubs do to develop that potential to elite levels?

Starting with the end in mind as suggested by Covey (1989) is important, but being able to anticipate what the outcomes of key performance match data in the future can only be at best guessed. A quote by M. Nakamura (1998; Toyota, Just-In-Time manufacturing method) warns that "only creatures that can respond to change will survive."

Of course those who anticipate change can better prepare themselves. From 1990 to 2005 there has been some interesting data in the physical/physiological and tactical elements of the game that have evolved with the introduction of rule changes, a more holistic approach to development and performance and the demands of the commercial world:

- Increased distances covered by all positions
- Increased distances covered at high speed
- Change in body type to muscular mesomorph
- Increased number and use of substitutes
- More teams keeping possession more frequently
- More goals scored from longer passing sequences

Table 6.1 shows position-specific technical data for Premier League players taken in the 2010/11 season to indicate the standard required to perform at this level.

Physical data produced by Prozone over the past three seasons in relation to average distance (kilometres) covered per team in the Premier League would suggest that the more successful teams are covering less overall distance. This could suggest that it is the high-intensity data that is more important given that it is in these moments that goals are created and scored or averted.

It may be difficult to partition learning effects from those with early growth and maturation, as they may appear to achieve tasks more easily.

In this next section we shall look at the different development age bands as defined by the EPPP but generally accepted for many years as the natural chronological ages for transition. We shall look at some of the rules and regulations of the EPPP and how these relate to what has been going on in other countries and what appears to be best practice.

A fundamental pillar of the EPPP is to facilitate more coaching time both during and after school hours to accumulate the sort of hours we see abroad and that has allowed countries like Holland and France to produce world-class international players consistently over the past 40 years. There has been a lot of research around practice time and how much is needed to become an expert or an elite performer. Ericsson

TABLE 6.1 Performance Benchmark – FA Premier League Positional Analysis, March, 2011

Attacker	March	Season
Total passes	23.7	24.2
Passing success %	80	79.1
Balls received	36.6	38.2
Ave. no. touches	2.13	2.11
Pen area entries	3.7	3.6
Headers	6.9	7.9
Crosses	1.6	1.5
Shots	2.8	2.9
Shots on target	1.6	1.6
Fouled	1.8	1.6
Tackles	1.7	1.9
Fouls	1.5	1.5

Left Midfield	March	Season
Total passes	33.8	31.5
Passing success %	82.5	80.3
Balls received	41.7	40.3
Passes forward	12.7	12
Ave. no. touches	2.65	2.55
Final 3rd entries	6.2	5.2
Pen area entries	6.7	6.3
Crosses	3.7	3.3
Shots	2.3	2.2
Fouled	1.7	1.6
Tackles	2.5	2.6
Fouls	0.9	0.9

Centre Midfield	March	Season
Total passes	43.4	43.8
Passing success %	82.7	83.6
Balls received	41.7	42.9
Passes forward	19.1	17.8
Ave. no. touches	2.01	2.03
Final 3rd entries	7.9	7.6
Pen area entries	3.9	3.7
Shots	1.2	1.2
Blocks	1.8	1.8
Interceptions	13.3	12.2
Tackles	4	4
Fouls	1.4	1.4

Right Midfield	March	Season
Total passes	31.7	31.3
Passing success %	80	80.4
Balls received	38.8	40.1
Passes forward	13	11.9
Ave. no. touches	2.53	2.47
Final 3rd entries	5.3	5.3
Pen area entries	5.7	6.7
Crosses	3	3.7
Shots	1.8	2
Fouled	1.2	1.3
Tackles	2.5	2.7
Fouls	1.3	1

Left Back	March	Season
Total passes	34.6	34.3
Passing success %	76.8	79.4
Balls received	34.5	34.5
Passes forward	19.5	18.5
Ave. no. touches	2.03	2.01
Final 3rd entries	9.2	8
Pen area entries	3.9	3.7
Crosses	2.1	2.3
Clearances	3.4	3.2
Interceptions	14.8	14
Tackles	3.6	3.2
Fouls	0.9	0.9

Centre Back	March	Season
Total passes	24.5	27
Passing success %	83.1	82.9
Balls received	21.1	23.5
Passes forward	12.7	14.6
Ave. no. touches	1.62	1.67
Final 3rd entries	4.4	4.5
Headers	12	12
Clearances	5.1	4.6
Blocks	1.6	1.8
Interceptions	21.2	20.9
Tackles	3.3	3.2
Fouls	1.1	0.9

Right Back	March	Season
Total passes	28.5	31.9
Passing success %	80	78.9
Balls received	28.9	32.2
Passes forward	14.5	16.5
Ave. no. touches	1.86	1.95
Final 3rd entries	7.1	7.3
Pen area entries	3.4	3.6
Crosses	2.2	2.4
Clearances	3.2	3.2
Interceptions	15.2	14
Tackles	3.4	3.3
Fouls	1	0.9

Goalkeeper	March		Season	
Saves	1.51		1.64	
Caught shots	1.81		1.61	
Caught crosses	1.12		0.92	
Punched crosses	0.3		0.28	
Caught corners	0.23		0.19	
Punched corners	0.14		0.27	
Caught freekicks	0.4		0.32	
Punched freekicks	0.07		0.14	
Goalkicks (avg. dist. M)	8.7	57.8	9.6	55.8
Freekicks (avg. dist. M)	4.5	48.6	4.5	48.1
Kicks from hands (avg. dist. M)	4.8	54.5	3.8	51.6
Throws (avg. dist. M)	4.6	24.3	5	24.3

Team Total Analysis (excluding GK)					
	March	Season		March	Season
Total passes	318	320	Headers	75	72
Passing success %	80	80	Tackles	31	31
Balls received	353	365	Fouls	12	12
Passes forward	143	146	Interceptions	124	119
Final 3rd entries	68	67	Crosses	16	16
Pen area entries	36	35	Shots	14	14

(1993) is probably the best known researcher in this area. His research suggests that it takes around 10,000 hours over a 10- to 12-year period to reach elite levels. However, his studies focused mainly on closed skills and cognitive skills and included musicians and chess players. Our research found that in leading professional football clubs around Europe, elite players were not gaining anywhere near the amount of practice time suggested from the Ericsson data (see the practice timetable below).

These exclude game time and are based on a 40-week season from under-9 through to under-19.

These coaching hours throw up some fundamental questions, such as what are the boys doing before they join at under-9 that might contribute to their expertise? Are they doing other things outside their coaching time that are contributing to their development as footballers? Is the type of practice critical to development?

TABLE 6.2 AJ Auxerre = 4,700 up to U19

Age groups	Practice sessions	Time per week	Time per year
U9–U11	3 × 1.5 hrs	4.5 hrs	180 hrs
U12–U13	5 × 2 hrs	10 hrs	400 hrs
U14–U15	5 × 2 hrs	10 hrs	400 hrs
U16–U19	8 × 2 hrs	16 hrs	640 hrs

TABLE 6.3 Ajax = 4,380 up to U19

Age groups	Practice sessions	Time per week	Time per year
U9–U12	3 × 1.5 hrs	4.5 hrs	180 hrs
U13–U15	7 × 1.5 hrs	10.5 hrs	420 hrs
U16–U19	10 × 1.5 hrs	15 hrs	600 hrs

TABLE 6.4 Bayern Munich = 3,900 up to U19

Age group	School sessions per week	Club sessions per week	Hours per season
U8		2 = 3 hrs	120
U9		2 = 3 hrs	120
U10		2 = 3 hrs	120
U11	2 = 2 hrs	3 = 4.5 hrs	260
U12	2 = 2 hrs	3 = 4.5 hrs	260
U13	2 = 2 hrs	3 = 4.5 hrs	260
U14	3 = 3 hrs	4 = 6 hrs	360
U15		7 = 12 hrs	480
U16		7 = 12 hrs	480
U17		7 = 12 hrs	480
U19		7 = 12 hrs	480
U23		7 = 12 hrs	480

TABLE 6.5 Bayer Leverkusen = 3,980 up to U19

Age groups	Practice sessions	Time per week	Time per year
U9–U11	3 × 1.5 hrs	4.5 hrs	180 hrs
U12–U16	5 × 2 hrs	10 hrs	400 hrs
U17–U19	5 × 2 hrs + 2 × 1 hr	12 hrs	480 hrs

TABLE 6.6 Feyenoord = 2,960 up to U19

Age groups	Practice sessions	Time per week	Time per year
U9–U10	2 × 1.5 hrs	3 hrs	120 hrs
U11–U12	3 × 2 hrs	6 hrs	240 hrs
U13–U19	4 × 2 hrs	8 hrs	320 hrs

TABLE 6.7 Barcelona = 2,760 up to U19

Age groups	Practice sessions	Time per week	Time per year
U9–U11	3 × 1.5 hrs	4.5 hrs	180 hrs
U12–U14	4 × 1.5 hrs	6 hrs	240 hrs
U15–U17	5 × 1.5 hrs	7.5 hrs	300 hrs
U18–U19	5 × 1.5 hrs	7.5 hrs	300 hrs

How does the structure of the sessions impact on development? This could be the basis for further study investigating the holistic biography of elite players, coaching practice and how other domains of sport science impact on their development.

To attain 10,000 hours over a 10- to 12-year period means training most days for three hours, and this could prove difficult to achieve for various reasons, not least the physical demands on the body at such a young age. If we consider time not spent on the grass training, such as performance analysis, mental skills training and other sport science support, we could perhaps get close, but it is hard to measure the efficacy of these support domains and how this sort of commitment impacts on players' domestic, social and academic worlds.

We often hear in the media, especially when the national team underperform or do not reach expectations, that English players lack the technical abilities of other countries. This has been highlighted in the previous World Cup of 2010 and the European Championship of 2012. This long-held criticism fuelled our desire to look closely at what the best clubs were doing in regards to their coaching practice.

Looking at the structure of the coaching sessions, generally we recorded that they had a 25%–75% emphasis on opposed practices to develop game craft and skills realistic to the game and its environment. Clubs expressed that they delivered unopposed technical sessions for individuals and small groups as part of individual development plans, but these were for short periods of time (15–30 minutes perhaps twice a week), and tended to be bolted on to sessions either prior or post the squad session. One of the observations of Academies' coaching practice in England has been that coaches have consistently spent too much time on technique/unopposed practices with the whole group and that players have then found it difficult to transfer that learning into the games. There seems to have been a misunderstanding when the foreign coaches talk about technique being the foundation of their development programmes because they then conduct skill/opposed sessions using that language. It isn't that our players aren't as technically gifted as our foreign competitors, but that we are not practiced enough in skill-based sessions to keep the ball, as it appears many English coaches have taken their spoken word literally and not looked at the consequences of learning the game.

. There was a real mixture of how the clubs facilitated their coaching plans. Some were very prescriptive like Bayern Munich, whilst others like Feyenoord allowed the coaches to develop their own ideas on how they create the practices to convey the key learning focus, but were on hand to help and guide them if needed. What also came out consistently was that the sessions were random and variable. One particular theme did not run throughout the whole session, especially with the younger players. For example, despite Bayern Munich being very descriptive about each theme, the sessions that we saw were very random and variable. They might include focus on a number of skills such as passing, shooting, dribbling and defending and tackling; these would usually be practised in a game situation.

It is very important to keep in mind that putting practice into action, and being able to evaluate a player's ability to transfer learning, can be a very subjective process. Assessing the efficacy of the training programme in competitive games versus real opposition is a vital part of development. The games programme for the majority of Academies is regionally based up to under-16 and does question the idea of the best playing against the best to develop the best. Some clubs, such as Ajax and Barcelona, play their boys against older boys to give them physical and mental challenges they have to find answers to. At AJ Auxerre, the Head of Academy Recruitment, Gilles Rouillon, believed that the strength of the opposition was not a major concern until players reach under-15 – then, in his experience, it became more important for the boys to be challenged more – and that having lots of success in the early years consolidates learning and builds self-esteem and confidence. The overriding philosophy at all the clubs was around development and not winning at all costs.

Foundation Phase (under-6 to under-11)

Most professional football clubs' development starts at the tender age of 5 via development centres. These centres are based within one hour's commuting distance from the main centre and are several in number, geographically placed in areas the club recognise there is a need based on their ability to hire a suitable venue, population, and socio-economic and historical criteria. These centres provide free football activities for anything from one session per week up to three sessions per week. Young boys who show an early ability for the game will be recommended by scouts, the football foundation staff and other contacts in the area and will attend one of these centres. Some kind of assessment will be conducted over an initial six-week period, and a decision is usually made to either invite them back for a subsequent period of time or release them back into grass-roots football. Up until their under-9 year, the boys and parents do not sign any formal contract, and therefore we often see boys attending more than one professional clubs' centre; parents need to be mindful of the dangers of overuse injuries, possible isolation from school peers and early specialisation.

The development focus is usually technique based with lots of work with the football, moving into skill-based work when opponents are introduced. There has been a lot of research (e.g. Drust et al., 2009) on what types of activities young footballers should be undertaking, and a lot of evidence suggests that a greater percentage of time should be devoted to skill-based activities that relate to the game, i.e. small-sided games from 1 v. 1 up to 5 v. 5. Ajax have used this format for many years and claim it is essential for the Foundation Phase for long-term development. Manchester United have also conducted their own studies on this playing format and have come to many of the same conclusions, the key ones being that it replicates the essence of the 11-a-side game, i.e. an invasion game. The players are constantly involved and therefore have to make lots of decisions both on and off the ball, which enhances technical skills, game craft and perceptual skills that guide motor and cognitive activity.

The Foundation Phase is often referred to as the 'golden age' of learning psycho-motor skills, as the brain appears to be more receptive at laying down neural pathways. It is therefore important that practice relates closely to the game in that it is directional, competitive and realistic. The small-sided games format fulfils these criteria and helps to create the environment that young players want to be involved in.

The Football Association have recognised that coaches who work with young players (5–21) need complementary training and qualifications, and in 2009 they launched the first of four modules that make up the Advanced Youth Licence, which is aimed at coaches who want to pursue a career in youth development. Module 1, 'Creating the Environment,' looks primarily at the social corner in its Long Term Player Development model. This focuses on areas such as socialisation, motivation, self-esteem and managing difference. Module 2 looks at 'Developing the Practice' and looks at how to build observational skills, as well as the rationale for using different types of practices. Module 3 looks at 'Developing the Player' and covers areas such as physical development and coach interventions and coaching styles. Module 4 is due to be launched in 2013 and will allow the coach to qualify as a specialist in one of three different age bands: 5–11, 12–16 and 17–21. Once qualified in one age band, they may wish to qualify in subsequent age bands over time.

Youth Development Phase (under-12 to under-16)

Orlick (2000) points out that to foster talent it requires a support environment where the focus is on competing to be the best you can be. Whilst this is essential for talent to reach its potential, it cannot guarantee this will occur. He also identifies three psychological elements that boys around 14 need to possess to get over the 'adolescent hump':

1   Self-determination
2   Perceived competence in relation to motor skills
3   Self-motivation

It is important that when you can't do something you have a determined mind-set to conquer it, as opposed to feeling a failure and being frightened of doing it again. We have come across staff who inculcate this mentality through their work with players on and off the training ground.

From an English perspective, the introduction of the EPPP should ensure that at least Category 1 and 2 clubs will have much greater access to the players. This will facilitate the delivery of education and sport science support and, crucially, allow coaches more time to work individually and collectively with the players. Expert opinion, research and theory around learning from across a range of performance domains all point towards the vital importance of being able to offer more support at this stage (see Table 6.8 below).

The Category 1 clubs will be expected to produce a diary that facilitates a rising scale from 10 hours per week for its under-12, under-13 and under-14 players to

TABLE 6.8 EPPP model for coaching hours by category of club

		Foundation Phase (Under-9 to Under-11)	Youth Development Phase	Professional Development Phase
Category 1	Coaching hours per week	4 rising to 8 for older Academy players	10 rising to 12 for older Academy players	14 reducing to 12 for Academy players who have commitments to the professional squad during the Professional Development Phase
	Permitted Training Model	Part-Time, Hybrid	Part-Time, Hybrid, Full-Time	Full-Time
Category 2	Coaching hours per week	3 rising to 5 for older Academy players	6 rising to 12 for older Academy players	14 reducing to 12 for Academy players who have commitments to the professional squad during the Professional Development Phase
	Permitted Training Model	Part-Time	Part-Time, Hybrid	Full-Time

(Continued)

TABLE 6.8 (*Continued*)

		Foundation Phase (Under-9 to Under-11)	Youth Development Phase	Professional Development Phase
Category 3	Coaching hours per week	3	4 rising to 6 for older Academy players	12
	Permitted Training Model	Part-Time	Part-Time	Full-Time
Category 4	Coaching hours per week	N/A	N/A	14 reducing to 12 for Academy players who have commitments to the professional squad during the Professional Development Phase Games Programmes
	Permitted Training Model	N/A	N/A	Full-Time

12 hours per week for their under-15/16 age groups. The Category 2 clubs will have a similar rising scale from 6 hours per week rising to 12 hours per week for their under-15/16 age groups. However, with this privilege comes the potential danger of 'burnout'. This term suggests that it is some sudden exhaustion or pivotal moment that a budding athlete encounters, whereas in reality it is an insidious condition brought on over time and often results in the athlete's self-perception of not being able to meet the physical or psychological demands of the sport. Although many factors can contribute to burnout, Balague (1999) suggests that three are very important: negative performance evaluations, inconsistent feedback from coaches and significant others and, finally, overtraining.

Professional Development Phase (under-17 to under-21)

The football development up to under-17 is very consistent, but from then on clubs had different ways to make the last transition into the professional environment. In Holland they tended to loan the players out, and the Feyenoord model seems to work well. Barcelona have a second team called Barca 'B,' which plays in the Segona 'A' Spanish league, and AJ Auxerre have two reserve teams rather than loan their players out. So each club has adopted a strategy to suit their needs. The new EPPP under-21 competition is going to encourage clubs to hold onto more of their players between the ages of 18 and 21 to compete in this league; this will greatly improve the standard of what will effectively be the old reserves league, but with the emphasis on developing players from within and being more particular about who they loan out to gain that first team experience. Some of the top English clubs have been keen to loan their young players out and charge loan fees, which could be detrimental to development.

Transitions from part-time schoolboy to full-time scholar at 16 years are going to be less demanding for the players involved with Category 1 and 2 clubs, as they will already be training most days already. Some boys will already be living away from home at an earlier age, and their education and welfare needs will have already been transferred to the responsibility of the club. However, they will still have to manage their time carefully as they juggle with a full-time training programme and 12 hours of academic education at college.

Sport science and medicine have made greater impact in professional football over the past 15 years than any other domain (Drust et al., 2009). From a medical point of view, it is about prevention and keeping players fit for longer, and with the support of complementary specialists helping to minimise the risk of injury and reduce rehabilitation times. We have gone from the 'sponge man' to highly qualified medical staff to cater for the physical consequences of the game, and from the coach trying to remember key moments in the game to performance analysis where every moment can be recalled. This has greatly enhanced the learning and focus of the players. We have seen more and more bespoke specialists being introduced to the support teams, who all have something to offer as clubs look more and more into margins that might make a difference.

Performance analysis

Performance analysis has grown tremendously in the last 10 years, where it initially supported the coaches in mainly match analysis. We now see it used far more widely and smartly. For example, footage and stats are used to review and address team, unit, player and coach actions in relation to the philosophy and game plan. This can range from set-pieces through to an individual player's objectives.

One area that has been highlighted by the book *Moneyball* by Michael Lewis (2003) is in the use of analytics for talent ID and recruitment. Billy Bean, the Oakland A's General Manager, used analytics to recruit baseball players who were seen as not good enough by the scouts and pundits but who fit within a budget and had a particular skill set capable of contributing to the team's philosophy. The Oakland A's were working on a budget of around a third of their main competitors and still managed to compete consistently at the business end of the season. A good example of this working in elite football was the rise of Bolton Wanderers from the Championship in 2001 to the Premier League under the management of Sam Allardyce (Gilmore and Gilson, 2007). Bolton were having serious money problems when they gained promotion, and although the promotion saved them financially, they were under tight budgets and therefore had to find a way of surviving with one of the lowest budgets in the Premier League. This was achieved by using the loan system and identifying players of quality who would fit into the playing philosophy and for some reason or another whose careers had stalled. Examples of these were Youri Djorkaeff, world cup winner; Ivan Campo, European Cup winner; Jay-Jay Okocha; Kevin Davies; and many more. Allardyce used a similar method to Billy

Bean, analysing performance data as part of his decision making. Bolton enjoyed an unprecedented spell of success, which culminated in them qualifying for the UEFA cup twice by finishing 6th in 2005 and 7th in 2007.

Analytics is now having an impact in many areas, including player and coach development, medical screening and specific areas such as biomechanics. For youth development programmes in England, one of the biggest challenges it faces with the EPPP will be to manage the data, make sense of it and help them make more informed decisions. There are a few companies who have been developing software over the past few years to support football clubs to manage their data, such as Sports Office and Edge10. These programmes are designed to help staff cross-reference and keep up-to-date biographies.

Performance analysis support appears patchy across the youth development centres visited abroad but is almost universal in English clubs. A good example of how a club has embraced this new technology is Ajax. When I first visited them in 2001 they had no performance analysis support, but when I revisited them in 2010 they had made great investment into it and most pitches at the training ground had cameras around them to provide in-depth analysis of coaches and players. The footage is stored on a server that all staff and players can access to embrace self-learning as well as directed learning. Other clubs offered no performance analysis support at all for their youth players. One centre had all the equipment and cameras needed to conduct analysis using Prozone software but did not have the staff trained to use it.

Strength and conditioning

All the clubs in our research and applied experiences employed strength and conditioning staff to help test and develop the players in this very important and measurable area of development. Explaining why this was highly valued, one club we visited expressed their philosophy as being about "creating an environment that challenges athletes physically and mentally to prepare them for the rigours of professional football". They viewed strength and conditioning as part of this because of the benefits it can provide directly in relation to playing performance, as an injury prevention intervention and, interestingly, to enhance psychological resilience. Staff believed that this psychological quality and mental skills like focusing, concentration and persistence would develop as the young players had to adhere systematically and fully to a demanding physical regime that could be very exhausting and uncomfortable and sometimes be perceived as boring.

Research undertaken by Nike in America studied the physical and physiological development of 14-year-olds over a four-year period and concluded that if athletes are serious about fulfilling their physical potential they need to be in the top quartile of athletes in their field by the time they are 18. Therefore, assessments and interventions made during this development phase need to be specific to the athlete. They have also gathered physical test data using the Sayers equation (Nele et al. 1999) to measure peak power in watts from English Academies over the two years from May 2010 to March 2012 and are starting to produce physical indicators that increase the likelihood of playing in a Premier League Academy as opposed to a lower league Academy. For example, under-18 forwards with an arrowhead agility score of 15.91 or lower are three times more likely to be playing at a Premier League Academy. This initial data also show that forwards are gaining higher SPARQ test scores throughout all the age groups from under-13 to under-18. The design of these tests does favour the players with explosive abilities, as we see most midfield players are gaining the lowest scores apart from goalkeepers but when looking at just the aerobic test they come out the best. Therefore, it is important to put these tests in context and to use them as part of the equation for player development.

Diet, nutrition and meals

The education around diet and nutrition has focused on balance for boys under 16. This is making players and parents aware of what a balanced diet looks like, what types of foods help with recovery within the first hour post-exercise and the importance of hydration and the types of fluids they should be drinking. Beyond 16 years clubs then start to focus on supporting the strength and conditioning work with diet and nutritional advice and supplements. It is also important for those players staying in home stays or club accommodations that the people providing the food are aware of players' diet needs and how best to prepare foods to retain their vitamin and mineral qualities. Some clubs put on cooking demonstrations for the parents and people who prepare the food for the players away from the club. A holistic perspective is taken at the best Academies; nutrition needs are seen in relation to the players' own specific needs rather than adopting a one-size-fits-all approach.

Most clubs measure the body fat percentage of players once they are full-time and set a standard that young players should be aiming for, which is usually under 10% by the time they reach 19 years. This is a vital part of the all-around strength and conditioning programme to prevent injuries, promote confidence and be able to compete in training and games.

The best clubs try to approach the question of diet and nutrition by creating an opportunity for players (and staff) to enjoy a meal after training each day. A meal is a social event of considerable importance; it is not merely about consumption of food but about informal interaction with others. Most centres had separated dining areas, or there were staggered times to eat so that each group had some level of exclusivity to allow in-group socialising. However, when the youth players were able to mix in with their senior colleagues, we saw this as a great opportunity for young players to integrate and ask questions that help towards the pathway to the top. The socialising aspect cannot be undervalued, and one spin-off of this was that when senior players were coming out early prior to the training session, we saw young players being asked to join in head tennis games or keep up games. The best clubs made considerable efforts to maintain this level of social interaction between the players and staff at Academy and first team levels. Most staff seemed aware of the importance of this. For example, in our applied work and research at the clubs, we heard about players who had become overcome by the stress and anxiety associated with the heightened de-socialisation (Fforde, 2009) that can often be experienced where players move up to join the first team squad. Clearly, the best clubs are trying to address this challenge, although they are not always successful.

Medical

Due to the rules and regulations of UEFA and their own national associations, all the centres have the required number of medical staff to support the boys in this area. Again the range of support was quite different. This ranged from what we found at Aspire, who have their own hospital on-site, to others where there is physiotherapy support, medical cover and quite modest facilities.

Medical screening is undertaken generally from around under 13 by some clubs as a preventative measure, taking particular interest in backs and pelvic areas. This is used most often for players they intend to sign on contracts but also for existing players to monitor growth spurts and for players who are in the readapting phase of their rehabilitation before joining the squad training.

Screening is also used to identify where there are strengths and weaknesses in body parts. For example, does a player have a leg length discrepancy? How does that affect the way he runs and walks? The use of film can slow these actions right down to identify which muscles need working on and other interventions that might be needed, such as orthotics or podiatry support.

Based on the research and our applied experiences, we would make the following recommendations:

1   Performance analysis and analytics can be used to support work at Academy levels. However, it is vital that players and staff are carefully educated to understand how to interpret this data to enhance learning and performance in football-related tasks.
2   Physical training is important, but more important is that it is specific to football.
3   Player nutrition is best addressed through employing specialist dieticians to ensure a holistic approach is taken to this important topic.
4   Opposed practices dominate all sessions at the best Academies. Unopposed sessions should be used much more sparingly. They have value where coaches need to avoid injury, introduce difficult and new technical or tactical interventions, or where fatigue is an issue.
5   The socialisation of players into the Academy and the club is not an optional extra. It is vital to ensure optimum performance and learning. Clubs should take this seriously and invest in staff and facilities to aid this process as fully as possible.
6   Clubs and Academies should operate with an agreed-upon, easily understood and clear ideal of the types of players they are looking for. This will assist the progress of players and ultimately benefit the first team.
7   The 10,000 hours rule must be interpreted with great care. It appears that the best clubs do far less formal work than this rule implies. It also seems to be that players are expected to find fun, informal and creative ways to take part in activities outside of the club that can improve their football-related competence. Intensity, passion, flow and immersion count more than total hours, programmes and systems. Quality, not quantity, is the maxim.

7

PSYCHOLOGICAL SUPPORT

Introduction

The impact of sport psychology in professional football has been much less than in many other sports. Some of the reasons for this are the nature of the sport, its culture and its attitude towards new ideas. In relation to this, Nesti (2010) has outlined the main challenges that sport psychologists have faced in working inside EPL clubs at first team levels. For example, problems around measuring the effect of sport psychology work on performance, finding time to do the work and gaining 'buy in' from players and staff are likely to be universal experiences. It can be argued that despite national and cultural differences, many of these obstacles exist throughout the sport, especially at professional and elite levels. In a British context there may be other particular difficulties to overcome, such as antipathy towards academic or scientific input, rejection of psychology as merely common sense or a belief that the coaches are able to cover the work of sport psychologists.

At youth levels and in the Academies, the type and range of challenges facing the sport psychologist may appear less. Ostensibly, there is or should be greater concern with the developmental aspects of the player, including their psychological growth (Gilbourne and Richardson, 2006). Youth coaches tend to devote a considerable amount of time to assessing players' attitudes, motivation and commitment. Although rarely done through use of scientific methods, the data gathered by the staff is used throughout the year to make decisions on team selection, type of support needed and ultimately whether to retain or release a young player. This collection and analysis of psychological data may be done in a rather *ad hoc* way. Nevertheless, it is valued by coaches because it is often the key information that first team and Academy staff will use to help them decide when a player is ready to progress to professional levels.

Within the more conducive environment of the Academy, one would expect to see frequent and extensive involvement of sport psychologists. As will be discussed, this does not seem to have occurred, even at some of the world's best football Academies. After so many years where little has happened, the blame for this situation, and we suggest that this is the appropriate word, must lie with all parties: with the clubs, governing bodies, universities and those offering sport psychology support. The clubs have largely failed to embrace sport psychology despite claiming that, ultimately, psychological factors are the most important in identifying those who 'make the grade' from those who do not (Richardson et al., 2004). The various governing bodies at national and international levels have tried to encourage clubs to take this side of the sport more seriously. This has been done through education and offering support on the ground. However, we contend that much of what is on offer does not meet the needs of players and staff at the clubs themselves. For their part, Universities have programmes at undergraduate and postgraduate levels in sport psychology and sport science that help train the applied practitioners of the future. These are often supported by accreditation schemes of various sorts to help prepare trainees to enter the world of performance sport as qualified psychologists. With a few notable exceptions (e.g. Liverpool John Moores University), courses are delivered by staff with limited experience working inside elite professional football clubs. This failing is compounded by a curriculum that tends to exclusively focus on mental skills training, rather than including material on culture, organisational psychology and counselling (Nesti, 2007). Lastly, there are consultants from a variety of academic and professional backgrounds who are active in the market offering a range of approaches to mental training in sport. Some of these individuals and companies are highly skilled and informed about sport psychology theory and principles; others offer superficial and inappropriate interventions based on limited knowledge.

The majority of clubs we have visited and worked within have been reluctant to embrace the work of sport psychologists. Research carried out by Pain and Harwood (2007) has suggested that this may be the result of football coaches and other staff having little awareness or understanding about sport psychology, how it can be used and the benefits it might bring. Although there is undoubtedly some merit in these findings, overall this work is problematic because it is based on data from an Academy at an English Championship Division team. In contrast, our work has been with higher level clubs, and in both first team and Academy environments. In our view there is often an excellent appreciation of the value of sport psychology in these clubs; the major concern seems to be around what sport psychologists offer and whether they will be able to fit into the culture of elite professional football. In this chapter we will explore this apparent paradox more comprehensively. The debate has sometimes been extremely polarised; we would argue that there has been far too much heat and not enough light. We believe that whilst clubs have legitimate concerns about academic sport psychology, the University and sport psychology profession are also able to point to failings in football. By discussing and analysing some of the key issues, we hope that it will be easier to identify a way forward that respects the concerns of each side and reveals some common ground and possible future synthesis.

We will not consider the role of consultants from outside of the academic and professional psychology bodies in this chapter. This would take us far from our main concern and add even more confusion to what is currently a complex picture. However, it is worth noting that in some of the best clubs there has been good use made of expertise from occupational psychology and clinical psychology to support the work of sport psychologists (where these exist) and the activities of coaches and other staff. When involved in this way we believe that external consultants, including those without sport psychology qualifications, can provide highly effective and useful support to the clubs in the Academy and first team environments.

Sport psychology in the dock

It is quite clear that something has gone badly wrong. In spite of sport psychology being accepted as an academic subject at a very large number of higher education establishments in a many countries, its influence on the world's biggest sport has been negligible. To understand this it is necessary to briefly look back at the history of sport psychology and closely examine the dominant approaches within this academic discipline. In some ways sport psychology has made great strides in becoming a respected and respectable area of study. Psychology has been offered as a subject at most Universities since the end of the Second World War. It is often forgotten that up until the later part of the 19th century, psychology was usually embedded in philosophy or medical science (Giorgi, 1970). The beginnings of academic sport psychology are most frequently located in the mid-1960s in Europe and North America. University courses in sport psychology only really began to appear in significant numbers in the 1980s. Usually embedded within multidisciplinary programmes like sport science, kinesiology or human movement, the first lecturers of this new discipline were often former physical education trained graduates, or coaches, rather than psychologists. This historical fact has had very profound influences on the subsequent development of theory and practice in sport psychology. One of the most important, it could be argued, was that with little in-depth knowledge of the parent discipline, the new breed of sport psychology staff tended to promote a cognitive approach to psychology, especially when it came to applied practice. Dominant since the 1970s in the Universities in the English-speaking world at least, this approach has the advantage of being easy to understand and even easier to apply through the use of cognitive-behavioural techniques. The enthusiasm for this naturally led to burgeoning research into the efficacy of cognitive interventions and examination of cognitive constructs like competitive anxiety. In a rarely acknowledged review, Nesti (2004) has highlighted how this unfortunate development resulted in an obsession with mental skills training and a tendency to view sport psychology only in terms of a limited number of approaches from the parent discipline of psychology.

An even more critical account by Corlett (1996a), which unfortunately has once again been largely ignored by the academic community, argues that sport psychology has frequently become synonymous with mental skills training. He makes the very important point that often techniques are taught to allow athletes to address symptoms, where a better approach would be to consider underlying causes. Corlett criticises sport psychologists for giving the impression that all uncomfortable feelings or strong emotions are bad and should be dealt with or removed. This is at best misleading, and at worst conveys the idea that achievement in sport is possible without experiencing difficult moments. In some ways this is similar to the work of Nesti (2010), which considers the use of existential phenomenological psychology at first team levels in the EPL. Existential approaches explain that anxiety can be a good sign because it often accompanies making choices, learning and development. A sport psychologist working from such a perspective would encourage the player to accept the feelings of anxiety or even embrace them since they are a positive sign that the person cares about the task in hand. Elite level coaches in football, including in the Academies, will know from experience that anxiety can be destructive on occasion, and at other times it will be viewed favourably by players. Traditional academic research in sport psychology took many years to discover this, which has done the discipline and applied sport psychologists few favours!

Another example of where sport psychology seems to have ignored reality and instead started from theory is in relation to mental toughness. Very few studies on this topic seem to commence without at first claiming that little is known about mental toughness in sport and amongst coaches. This absurd statement was based on the spurious argument that because coaches and others could not provide a satisfactory and comprehensive definition of mental toughness, it could only be because they did not understand it. This is somewhat equivalent to saying that because personality cannot be easily and succinctly defined and explained, that is evidence that there is no such concept. Such a narrow and restricted view about knowledge and understanding has hardened attitudes in clubs. At a number of clubs there was a view that sport psychologists do not seem able to accept that most support staff have good understanding of psychology. The following quotation from an experienced member of the coaching staff at a very successful club aptly summarises this point:

> We don't work with sport psychologists as extensively as we would like partly due to their failure to acknowledge that staff in football clubs possess in depth knowledge of many important psychological matters. This is based on their craft knowledge and experience; just because something cannot be articulated easily or presented in a more systematic way does not mean it is not well understood. The common complaint is that sport psychologists tell us about things we already know about; we want them to help us with areas that are beyond our knowledge or where we lack the professional competence to act.

Clubs in denial

A frequently mentioned impediment to involving sport psychologists was that there were insufficient resources to allow this to happen. Where clubs did have money to spend, it was often used to recruit players or appoint additional staff. As we have seen and heard over many years, when Academy Directors and heads of youth pro-grammes have additional finance for staff recruitment, they have tended to appoint more coaches. This is similar to what takes place at first team levels. The main exception to this is where a club feels they do not have sufficient medical support, and therefore they may be prepared to take on more physiotherapy and physical therapy expertise. In recent years, elite clubs have begun to add strength and con-ditioning, fitness and performance analysis staff at Academy levels. For example, at Ajax we noted that they had increased their personnel in these support areas by over 300% in just the last 10 years. And yet with very few exceptions, this growth has not been evident in sport psychology support at youth levels (Nesti and Littlewood, 2009).

Where clubs did have some support it was often part-time or provided by out-siders on a consultancy basis. We saw examples where this appeared to work well. This might have been due to the skills of the sport psychologists, the attitudes of the coaches and the culture of the club. For example, at Ajax, and in our own experi-ence at Bolton Wanderers in the English Premier League, two part-time sport psy-chology staff were employed to great effect at the Academy, and a further one with the first team supported by a full-time senior sport psychologist at the club. Despite the success of this approach and the recognition it received in the game across the world, we have never come across anything like this level of commitment to sport psychology provision at any other club.

Our findings point towards the crucial role that the first team manager can play in supporting sport psychology in the Academy. It is this person, sometimes sup-ported by a performance director, who must convince the CEO that resources must be found to employ sport psychology staff. They have the influence to ensure that suitable contracts in terms of pay, hours and conditions of service are applied to the employment of sport psychologists at the club. Even in those situations where the Academy Manager has considerable financial autonomy, leadership from the top will be vitally important. This is because the natural instinct of most coaches, coupled with the fact that many are former players, is that coaching on the pitch must be the overriding priority. Anything that can potentially take resources in terms of money and time away from this activity will be resisted initially at least. This was described to us by some coaches at the clubs we visited as being a major obstacle to increasing sport psychology support. The view expressed was that if the choice came down to recruiting another coach or a full-time sport psychologist, most would opt for a coach. This indicated that the sport psychologist role was still seen as something of a luxury, and somewhat peripheral to the main task. This was summed up by one senior staff member at Bayer Leverkusen who pointed out that in order to satisfy the hours required to achieve expert performance levels, greater time needed to be devoted to playing and practice – this type of activity is led by coaches, not sport psychologists!

Clubs and coaching staff in particular are often unsure about how sport psychol-ogists can be effective in their work. This is because, unlike all other activities and roles, sport psychologists rely overwhelmingly on verbal and written communication to do their work. This is especially challenging with young people and is dependent on the ability to build trust and the readiness of the players to engage in dialogue. The sport psychologist is very likely to use group sessions and confidential one-to-one meetings, sometimes of quite an informal style, to overcome these challenges. These approaches can make the work of the sport psychologist easier to access and therefore more effective; the problem remains, though, of the less visible nature of much of this work and how to assess its impact.

The topic of measurement is always a contested area in psychology (Kuhn, 1977). Sport psychology is no different. One side argues that as a science sport psychology must be able to provide robust and rigorous data upon which decisions can be made with confidence. In opposition, some would claim that, given its subject matter is the human, it is both unrealistic and unnecessary to look for this level of certainty. This latter, more balanced view is usually the most common view inside the best clubs. They are highly critical of the dominant perspective in academic sport psychology that is more concerned with providing neat and tidy quantifiable results than in offering broader feedback based on an eclectic mix of hard and soft data.

A further concern of the clubs is around how measurements are to be used. At the best Academies there is often an unwritten policy that the club will decide what they should measure and how this should be done. This decision is important to get right because time and other resources are finite. Although by no means the same in every elite club we visited, the general pattern is one where substantially increased attention is directed at continual recording of player data. In some countries the club has less autonomy about specifying what they should record and how often this is done. In England the recently launched EPPP is very clear about what must be carried out. The result of this desire to measure has meant that very few aspects of a young player's development are not documented and scrutinized; this includes technical, physical and psychological elements. This is of course a huge demand on the time of staff. The next few years will tell if this is a productive use of staff expertise and resources; however, as far as sport psychology is concerned, the best Academies in the world do not operate in this way. There is little evidence that they record psychological data, and they are reluctant to devise ways to allow this to take place. In the English context, the EPPP clearly documents the types of psychological information that must be kept on players at youth levels. The usefulness of this data, and questions about the time required to collect, collate and analyse it, will be answered by the clubs in England in the next few years. If coaches and other staff do not feel that the psychological material they must record as part of the EPPP process is helping their work, the involvement of sport psychologists in clubs will come under further scrutiny. Through our research and applied experiences, we have observed that some clubs are becoming frustrated at the amount and kind of psychological information they are required to provide as part of the EPPP. It would be a very unfortunate situation if sport psychology provision in the English Academy context fails to expand due to concerns about the relevance, validity and sheer volume of measurements being carried out into players' psychological development.

One of the dangers arising from this philosophy of measurement and so-called evidence-based practice (Andersen, 2005) is that there may be a drift towards doing only things that can be objectively assessed, and away from tasks that are less easy to quantify. We can see this happening across professional football at the highest levels, especially with the growth in match analysis, player analytics and physiological data. It can only be hoped that clubs understand that much of the most powerful psychological information cannot be accessed the same way as in other scientific disciplines. Fortunately, sport psychology is not alone in this. Coaching also has to rely to a great extent on data that is not amenable to objective, quantifiable measurement. In fact, many of these more subjective and personal factors are important in both sport psychology work and coaching. Here we are referring to narrow psychological matters like focus, concentration, emotional control and motivation, for example. The list would also include character, personality, courage and spirit. In our work it was these types of psychological factors that were often mentioned to us as being ultimately the most important in player achievement. The coaches frequently mentioned these words and were usually very clear that it was the sport psychologist's role to address these. Even at the best clubs this remains the view, despite the fact that coaches are aware that they are involved (with other staff) in developing these and other psychological characteristics in their players. Therefore, we have the unusual but very common experience of clubs and coaches acknowledging the vital importance of developing the psychological side in their players, whilst expecting that the sport psychologist, as the expert, will be able to achieve this outcome on their own. It seems that the best clubs know that this view does not make sense theoretically, and is impossible in practice. And yet despite this, such a view is commonplace even at the best clubs we have experienced. This confused thinking about the realistic role for the sport psychologist has been yet another barrier to their greater involvement in professional football, even at the most forward thinking and successful clubs in the world.

Although used commonly in elite professional football, terms like character, personality and spirit are less frequently seen in modern academic sport psychology because they are difficult to quantify, and most likely because they seem more like philosophical terms. Sport psychology research has attempted to overcome this partly through validating various psychometric tests to measure mental toughness, motivation, anxiety or confidence (Williams, 2006). Although some of the data from these inventories could be useful, staff at the best clubs appear to be much better educated about the failings of trait approaches, as well as the lack of ecological validity and poor reliability of sport psychology psychometrics. As a result, decisions on players' futures, how they can be assisted and the best way to work with them as individuals tend to be based on information gathered in a more *ad hoc* and subjective way by staff at the clubs. In some ways this could be likened to longitudinal qualitative research methodology. The focus is on patiently building up a picture of a young player by careful observation, sustained dialogue and constant reflection. At the best clubs there is a recognition that this type of 'data' is harder to record and is infused with subjectivity. Despite these limitations, the most effective coaches appear to trust this information, as it seems better able to fit the complex world of professional football and represents a more meaningful approach to understanding player progression and development.

Where sport psychology has been conceived solely in terms of mental skills training (MST) and measuring psychological factors through the use of sports-specific psychometrics, the result has been to make it harder for sport psychologists to become accepted and valued full-time members of staff at clubs. In our applied practice and research, we heard time and again that the most experienced Academy staff are looking for something beyond MST from their sport psychologists. This is because they know through their work that the players face a range of challenges during their period as Academy players and must pass through many critical moments (Nesti and Littlewood, 2011) that require something other than the effective use of mental skills. Although clubs are aware of this need, few, with the exception of Bolton and Feyenoord, have been able to convert this understanding into a policy to guide their recruitment of sport psychology support.

Finally, the tendency to rely on part-time staff to deliver sport psychology was something we have encountered at all the clubs, for example, at Feyenoord and Bayer Leverkusen. This suggests that although clubs are convinced about the importance of psychology, they are less enthusiastic about the work of sport psychologists. Although as we have alluded to above, sport psychology – especially that practiced in the Universities – must share some of the blame for this, the clubs have not fulfilled their responsibilities here either. The level of understanding about the psychological area is highly developed in many of the coaching, education, welfare and other support staff at Academy levels. In contrast, there is little clarity about what a good sport psychologist should do in their role, and how they can justify their work (Anderson et al., 2004). Clubs seem to have ignored this issue and are only now beginning to think more carefully about the role and job descriptions. In England, the EPPP has helped to move this along, although we are still awaiting a more detailed account of how the sports psychologist should operate and what they must attend to.

Although this situation of uncertainty and lack of clarity is unfortunate, it does mean that there is now a very real opportunity to focus on this area of provision. This can also be carried out with the advantage of being able to consider this work in relation to the other forms of support in the clubs. In this way, clubs can develop an approach that meets the needs of the young players and that is designed to fit into an increasingly complex interdisciplinary environment.

The view of the coaches will be central to how the role of the sport psychologist is developed and evolves. This is because, as we have argued, the proficient coach must also be a sound psychologist. It is also the case that psychological factors impact on the work of all staff to some degree. Their views on what is required and how best to deliver this will be valuable. Chaplains, medical personnel, welfare officers and education staff are just some of those whose input could help ensure that the right kind of psychological support can become available to all Academy players.

A new way forward

In our many years working and researching in professional football, we have rarely come across any topic that generates so many competing and even contradictory views than that of sport psychology. This ranges from those who see this as something for weak individuals and those with mental health problems, to others who believe that psychological support will be most useful with the best – the high achieving, dedicated and focused elite player. Despite this apparent confusion, we feel that there is every reason for hope. At the very best of clubs, we heard time and again that the psychological factors were almost invariably the most influential on deciding how far a young player would go in the game. Staff told us about how keen they were to find the right individuals who could use their psychological knowledge and skills to enhance the work of the Academy. There was also a constant expression of genuine frustration about sport psychology being so well received in other sports and across the academic world, whilst continuing to have comparatively little impact in elite club Academy football.

Sport psychologists do at last seem to be getting the message that their function in professional football may be quite different than what has been envisaged to date. Even in research studies there have been some notable and important shifts. For example, a recent study by Cook et al. (2014) on mental toughness at one of the world's most successful football clubs revealed that Academy coaches possessed considerable understanding about mental toughness and how this can be developed. As we have already mentioned, this is in direct contradiction to many earlier studies on this topic which assert that mental toughness is little understood in the world of sport practice (Crust, 2007). At a deeper level, this statement reveals a failure to distinguish between the language used in sport and by coaches from the concepts and constructs used by researchers in their studies. This can be seen in so many areas of sport psychology research, where academics have made the illogical assumption that when a psychological concept is not described in terms familiar to them, it signifies that it is unknown in the world of practice. Such an error leads to misunderstanding between the sides, and a tendency to dismiss each other's views without careful and proper consideration. Not that this can be taken to mean that sport psychology research is redundant or worthless. On the contrary, it highlights that good research can offer much to assist the understanding of coaches. It can provide additional insights and interpretations, but in a more focused and specific way.

All of this discussion around research and theorising may seem to be of little concern to clubs when considering the provision of sport psychology. We would suggest that this is wrong. One of the main objections to employing full-time sport psychologists we came across centred on perceptions that they do not accept that other staff have extensive psychological knowledge. This is usually gained from life experience rather than academic study, and may be expressed in everyday language rather than psychological terminology. The view was that unless and until sport psychology and the psychologists come down from their ivory towers, the very important input they could offer in the Academies will be overlooked.

The coaches and others in the clubs must also be prepared to accept that sport psychology cannot be a panacea for all the difficulties they encounter. Sometimes the real problem is more about the culture (Wilson, 2001) that exists in the club, organisational dynamics and systems. For this change to take place there needs to be a realistic appreciation of what sport psychologists can be expected to address, where and when their skills will be most useful and how these link to the work of other staff. This is something we have seen that is currently happening at the best clubs, and in England has been encouraged by the EPPP process. Several top clubs that we visited or have worked with are now taking steps to appoint the people they want to provide the psychological support they need. This more strategic and carefully thought-through approach is likely to benefit the clubs by aiding them in getting the types of people they require who will be able to offer a service that is welcomed and valued. It will also go some way towards improving the negative perception that many professional football coaches have of sport psychology and sport psychologists.

One of the key differences that we found between the best clubs and others is that the coaching staff are frequently highly skilled in using sport psychology within their practices. At lower level clubs it is more usual to find coaches whose approach and knowledge is less sound. This has been reported by Brown and Potrac (2009) in their study into Academy football in England. They found that at many lower league clubs there exists a climate of fear and a culture of intimidation, where young players are poorly supported from a psychological point of view. We know that at elite clubs Academy coaches are constantly engaged in teaching mental skills techniques through their work with young players on and off the pitch. For example, maintaining a positive mentality after negative feedback or mistakes, how to set appropriate goals, the importance of emotional control and focus are just some of the types of skills that coaches incorporate in their work. This can take place on or off the pitch and is delivered formally, or included as part of coaching sessions. The programmes at Bolton and Feyenoord were fine examples of where clubs had embraced this fully. At all of the clubs we have seen, staff were keen to reiterate that they were looking for sport psychologists to assist in carrying out work aimed at developing greater use of psychological skills. Sometimes this will mean delivering a mental skills training programme directly to young players, often in small group sessions. On other occasions it requires the sport psychologist to work through the coach to support them as they take the lead on mental skills training. For example, at Feyenoord we saw the sport psychologist taking players through a very basic and fun introduction to the use of mental imagery and concentration skills. At these same clubs, sport psychologists were employed part-time to develop these and other mental skills in one-to-one, individually tailored sessions with more senior players in the Academy.

Beyond the mental skills role we saw sport psychologists beginning to take on the more organisational psychology type function that, as Nesti (2010) has noted, is well received at first team levels in the English Premier league. This work involves improving communication across and within departments and helping to create an environment that is conducive to high level performance. Nesti and Littlewood

(2009) have referred to sports psychologists carrying out this role as being a type of 'cultural architect'. These are individuals whose task is to help the formation and development of a very specific environment where interdisciplinary work is possible, innovation is welcome and highly skilled staff unite to form a dynamic and high performing team. This can additionally help to establish the optimum conditions for individual and group-based sport psychology work with players. This is because in many clubs, organisational stress represents a major source of negative challenges for both players and staff alike. This has been supported by research from Fletcher and Wagstaff (2009) and in high level sport by Cruickshank et al. (2014). They found that organisational issues were often the most important stressors faced by athletes. At a small number of the best clubs we know, the sport psychologist is involved in trying to reduce the effects of organizational stress to enhance performance of the group, and maximize the impact that any individual psychological support work will have.

Much of what the best clubs do in this area is geared towards giving players individual support. However, a lot of good work can be done in group sessions. These can be delivered in classroom settings, on the training ground or in more informal venues. Especially with very young players this seems to be the preferred way of teaching mental skills. With older age groups a mixed approach is used. For example, at the EPL clubs we have worked in the sport psychologist carries out whole team, smaller group-based and individual work. The one-to-one engagement can be informal and *ad hoc*, or more planned and formal. Very few clubs have a specific area identified for individual sessions on sport psychology. This is a surprising failing and could be interpreted as reflecting a less than committed view about the importance of sport psychology. From a professional practice perspective, it could also make it harder to ensure confidentiality and may make players less prepared to engage in an open and in-depth dialogue. This can be particularly important with the older players, where topics can range from concerns about being released and communication problems with the coach or other staff to parental pressure and worries about securing a professional contract (Andersen, 2005).

The best practice we have encountered across Europe at clubs like Feyenoord is where the sport psychologist conceives their role to be about performance enhancement and player well-being. For example, one senior coach at Feyenoord commented that in their opinion the sport psychologist must always be seen as someone a little different because they will often be sought by players during difficult professional and personal moments. On these occasions the empathy and compassion shown by the psychologist may be the most important factor they can contribute to help the young player. Where this is carried out carefully and with skill, such work could also positively impact performance as well as well-being.

Our research points towards the need for sport psychologists to operate holistically. This can be justified on a number of different levels, although two stand out as most convincing. First, sport psychologists, like all other staff at the Academy, are employed to help the club develop more and better players for the first team. This is the fundamental goal of any Academy and must always be borne in mind. Second, in order to assist players in improving their psychological skills and progress success-fully through the ranks, it is important that the sport psychologist is able to work with the whole person, not just the footballer. This is because, especially at older ages, some of the biggest challenges will be about broader non-sport issues. These can impact the player as much as, and in some situations even more than, football-related concerns. Players are less likely to discuss these broader life issues with the sport psychologist if they detect that the sport psychologist doesn't care about them as a person. This does not mean they must become friends, since this can interfere with the learning process. However, as we have witnessed in the best clubs, the most effective sport psychologists are those who are able to bring some compassion, empathy and care to their practice (Ravizza, 2002).

However, not everyone agrees with this perspective. The academic sport psy-chology community seems unsure about whether this type of philosophy can be applied in real-world practice. For example, Brady and Maynard (2010) argue that sport psychologists should concern themselves only with performance, whilst Andersen (2009) contends that caring for the athlete should be the sole focus. Nesti et al. (2012) have argued against both of these positions. This is based on a particular theoretical perspective allied to extensive applied sport psychology experience at the highest levels of professional football. In agreement with what we heard at Fey-enoord and Ajax, Nesti et al. (2012) and Mitchell et al. (2014) suggest that beyond learning how to use mental skills more effectively, much of what the sport psy-chologist encounters relates to supporting players in dealing with negative criticism and disappointments, managing behaviour on and off the field and building a clear self-identity. This can be achieved through counselling-type sessions (Andersen and Tod, 2006) involving dialogue aimed at developing greater self-awareness and self-knowledge. Ultimately, it is these final two elements that will help the young player to deal with the demands of being a teenager, entering young adulthood and accepting more responsibility for their own progression to full professional levels.

A final word on how clubs would like sport psychologists to carry out their work in Academy settings. All of the top clubs expect their sport psychologist to use a planned, systematic and more formal approach alongside an *ad hoc*, more reactive and informal way of working. There did not appear to be any strong views about how this balance should be maintained, or whether the psychologist should adapt this depending on the age and stage of the players. Academy staff were very clear that the players must be made aware that when they meet with the sport psycholo-gist on an individual basis, full confidentiality will be assured. They emphasized that because of the challenges and misperceptions that can exist around psychology, it is essential that group-based sessions do not resemble anything like school lessons. The sport psychologist must be highly skilled in presenting material in a way that is fresh, stimulating and enjoyable if they are to succeed.

Based on the research and our applied experiences, we would make the follow-ing recommendations:

1   Sport psychology must be about much more than mental skills training if it is to meet the needs of players in the Academy.

2   Sport psychologists must be skilled and sufficiently qualified to deal with broader concerns that are directly or indirectly football related. Dealing with these issues will often impact player performance more than teaching or improving mental skills.

3   There is a very important role for sport psychologists to act as organisational psychologists. This type of work will enhance performance across the Academy and help provide a culture of excellence to support individual player progression.

4   In order for points 1–3 to be addressed, academic sport psychology needs to realign its curricula to bring it closer to the reality of performance sport environments. At present, far too much research and theorizing is guided by the demands of academia, rather than the needs of user groups and consumers.

5   Sport psychologists who wish to be successful delivering support in professional football must offer a performance *and* a caring agenda at all stages of young players' development.

6   The sport psychologist should use a mix of delivery styles and formats ranging from formal to informal, and from planned to *ad hoc*, to meet the specific circumstances and culture that exist in the club.

7   Finally, sport psychologists should utilise the fact that other staff at the Academy will have considerable psychological knowledge. They must remember that good coaches are very often excellent psychologists. The success of the sport psychologist will depend on building on this *and* being able to contribute something extra to that which already exists.

8

CONCLUSION

In this chapter, we will first attempt to summarise the most important findings from our research and applied experiences in the game. These are not in order of importance, although there is little doubt that some will make a greater impact than others to the success of an Academy. In structuring the conclusion, we have been guided initially by the chapter headings and section titles. Beyond the detail, however, it seems to us that there are some key underlying messages that are clearly discernible when one looks at the data. One of these is that the staff are the most important resource in creating highly effective centres for the development of young footballers. This is not a new or surprising finding; it has been said many times before and is rarely disputed. It has long been acknowledged that high-quality coaching is absolutely necessary to produce elite performance. Clubs must appoint coaches with the best skills, most advanced knowledge and highest levels of motivation to want to develop. We often hear clubs talk about people being their greatest asset but then become very hesitant to support them with continual professional development. This may be borne out of the fear of losing good people, but what happens if you don't invest in them and they become systematic soldiers and stay!

Vocation

However, we think our work has found something to add to this well-known set of requirements. And that something is best captured by a rather old-fashioned word: vocation. This is a very specific and exact term. We used to speak commonly about someone having a vocation for something. There was always an understanding that in a very profound and clear way, possessing a vocation was not the same as doing a job, or following a career. A vocation is quite unlike a job or career because it always involves our whole selves. This may appear to be a strange statement, which sounds unnecessarily idealistic, as well as impractical and unobtainable. In fact, it is nothing of the sort, since it is, or at least was until recently, the term applied to a number of the most esteemed professional jobs possible. It was usual practice to speak of someone's vocation for the religious life, medicine, nursing, teaching and the law. These occupations were reserved for people who felt they had a calling to a particular way of life. The quasi-religious language that was often used to describe a vocation may have served to obscure the most fundamental feature shared by this wide range of jobs – each emphasised the importance of morality in pursuing its aims. Or, to express this in another way, a vocation is about the person doing their work within a moral framework – one that guides them to do the right thing rather than the thing required.

It is this quality that we discovered at the best Academies in the world. Sometimes difficult to identify and always impossible to measure, it is easy to see in the work people do and hear in the language they use. When staff at a football Academy see their work in terms of it being a vocation, we see people who care deeply about everything they do or say. They may not always make the best decisions and at times will even be guilty of serious failure; however, those with a vocation will always take it personally! This means that these individuals bring a level of commitment and motivation to their roles that is beyond what is reasonable to expect. They are fully immersed in the work and, in one sense, are always on duty. Thoughts are constantly turned to how to improve things, and what they could have done better. Such staff do not easily recognise the concept of the normal working day or week and will put in the hours needed to carry out their tasks. In addition, they are always ready to reflect on themselves, evaluate their achievements and consider any failings.

The best Academies carefully recruit such individuals to work in all departments. Mostly they get this process right. When they fail and appoint the wrong people, they act quickly to remove staff. Apart from this difficult task, there appeared to be few drawbacks to having large numbers of staff with a strong vocation on the team. The major problem seemed to be one facing management in getting individuals to take a rest and refresh themselves. However, we have noticed that many of these exceptionally skilled sports scientists, coaches and others are often engaged in a number of other activities and roles beyond their professional calling. They seem capable of being committed to a number of different identities simultaneously, without this lessening their passion and love for their work in football.

Identity

Turning away from the staff, we have seen how identity is so vital to the ongoing achievement of the best Academies. This is usually something that is shared across the club at different levels and extends out of the club to the local community or region. We heard repeatedly from players, coaches, administrators and others about the need to sustain the identity of the club – to become immersed in its values, traditions, history and culture. This was described in a number of very powerful ways. Coaches were especially keen to tell us that they were guardians of the club identity. Their role was to ensure the next group of players for the first team would continue the legacy. These staff could explain the philosophy of the club and, crucially, describe in considerable detail how this could be inculcated with the young players in their charge.

Identity was viewed as something permanent but that would always evolve over time. This perspective was best expressed by one Academy director who pointed out that "as a dynamic process, evolution could be shaped and guided to ensure it added to the clubs genotype. Our task is to add our little bit extra to help us become a more complete and more advanced version of ourselves."

Finally, it is very impressive to spend time inside clubs and find out that the best possess an identity that is at once visible to outsiders yet subtle in application, and understood by all but owned by none. The outstanding examples of this were Barcelona, Bayern and to some extent Ajax. However, it is fair to say that all the clubs in the research without exception had unique, vibrant and powerful identities that were loved by fans and feared by opponents.

Investment

The European sports club model appears to allow football decisions to be made in the best interest of the whole club, and youth development is a major part of this. Often in England when clubs are looking to save money the first budget to be slashed is the Academy budget. This will be more difficult for English clubs to do in the future and will be a process as opposed to a whim so that as much of the quality and goodwill can be saved.

The foreign emphasis on developing players for their national teams has a consequence of also developing world-class players for their club teams. Maybe Holland and France in particular see themselves as selling nations because they do not command the commercial power that some other nations do, and this is reflected in the number of French players playing in the top five leagues in Europe (Professional Football Players Observatory [PFPO] annual report on player migration in the top five leagues 2010).

Budgets in Europe for their Academies show that they have consistently invested more than those in England in the past as a percentage of gross turnover and often as raw investment figures. This obviously states an intention and focus on what the clubs' priorities are; however, we are now seeing investment that is more competitive due to the new EPPP rules.

Leadership

The fact that the Academy Director/Manager reports into senior management or a board member reduces the chance of constant change, which is potentially very disruptive to a child's development.

Many of the Academy Directors/Managers had been in post or been involved in youth development for many years, and the most successful clubs and associations (Clairefontaine (French National Centre), Bayern Munich and Middlesbrough) have had the same person for between 13 and 30 years. One of many negative points that arise from constant change is the club invariably lose the talent they have in their system to other clubs, and that is being made even more accessible given the new rules on compensation.

If we broaden our research into the most productive Academies at Premier League level in England (Manchester United, Arsenal and West Ham; Professional Football Players Observatory 2010), we see stability in the Academy personnel and a clear playing philosophy.

The travelling time rule in England does appear to hinder the recruitment of quality players from a distance and reduces or waters down the quality at each club because the chances of getting enough good quality players working together are reduced. The relaxing of this rule in the new EPPP for Category 1 clubs and the new compensation packages are going to encourage these clubs to maintain high standards in their development programmes and perhaps get closer to the adage of the 'best with the best' and provide the type of environment where talent can flourish even more.

Player recruitment

Looking at the recruitment situation in England, we see that Manchester United, Arsenal and West Ham all reside in densely populated areas but are also some of the most competitive. Therefore, other factors such as the stature of the club, the quality of its staff and facilities and the philosophy of the club to promote young players can also have an impact on recruitment. The more sophisticated testing of trialists at 14 upwards is obviously trying to reduce risk and therefore costs. The triangulation of information to better inform Academy staff about their players is refining talent ID and development programmes.

The club link strategy appears to be a very good way of gaining access to talented boys, loaning young professionals to gain first team experience whilst players who are deemed not good enough can be offered back or sold on with profits shared. Part of the relationship also allows the parent club to allow access to all its other support operations like coach education, sport science and medical resources to the link clubs for their own development.

They nearly all expressed a formal or informal link with Africa, and some centres reflected this in their ethnic make-up.

Shared site

Most of the clubs had shared sites for the first team and Academy staff and players. This was one of the most talked about features in our research study. Senior staff in particular were very clear about the benefits of this type of arrangement. We heard about logistical, financial and organisational advantages. There was much made of the importance of being able to share equipment, pitches and training areas. Although these topics emerged almost everywhere, it was noticeable that some of the strongest clubs in terms of international and domestic achievement offered another major positive about the value of shared sites. Staff at these venues mentioned frequently that the most important factor was that this allowed for the development of a common culture to be created – one that covered every age and level and included all players and staff. This allowed for the inculcation of a particular playing style and helped staff and players to feel that they were an integral part of the club's performance and future success. The importance of this should not be underestimated because, as we were told repeatedly, everything must ultimately be measured in relation to how it helps first team results. An Academy that does not ensure this philosophy is fully understood by everyone is to be an Academy under threat! However, the best clubs also strived to maintain constancy with their cultures during difficult phases such as managerial changes, poor results or financial challenges. They did this because the template was well understood, associated with previous success and could be seen clearly on and off the training pitch.

The capacity to inspire younger players and assist more senior groups to see themselves as part of something much bigger and more important than their own concerns was mentioned repeatedly. The shared site represented the tangible and visible reminder of this.

We were impressed by how often staff talked about how the existence of a shared site engendered a family feel at the club. A closer interrogation of this revealed that staff were talking primarily about communication. It was pointed out that there is less opportunity for communication breakdown and misunderstandings to occur when all parties are at the same location. A further advantage was that informal sharing of information and rapid decision making was easier in this situation. This was described by Stanley Brard at Feyenoord, who pointed out that

> one of the big benefits to us is that we can behave like a close family where there are lots of ad-hoc and direct conversations taking place across departments and between people. This speed and accuracy is essential in our incredibly fast moving football environment.

Although we have come across some high level clubs where the Academy is not on the same site, this is quite rare. For example, as far back as 2005, research carried out by Littlewood suggested the most productive Academy clubs in England at the time were those who were based on the same site. The outlier to this was Manchester City. In contrast, clubs like Manchester United, Everton and Middlesbrough are all based on one site. It seems that most of the elite clubs agree with the sentiment expressed by one very experienced Academy manager we have worked with in the EPL: "One site, one mind!"

Culture of learning

It was quite striking how often we heard Academy staff talking about the importance of ensuring that, from the youngest to the more senior players, all needed to play the game with a similar philosophy. Part of the new EPPP criteria is for clubs to have an agreed-upon philosophy to guide process and practice across all levels at the club. Although the way this was achieved was adjusted to meet the developmental needs of the players, it was remarkable to see how the underlying philosophy of play was enforced and encouraged throughout matches, training and off-field behaviour. The details covered mentality, technical requirements, tactics and ways of playing. The best clubs have identified a 'way of being' – a personality that is easily discernible in very different contexts and situations. Staff unity around this is complete; there is a sense of deep pride and commitment to their DNA. This ensures that when players progress they move within a familiar framework, helping them to deal with the escalation in performance expectations and greater focus on winning and results.

In terms of playing styles there was general agreement that it is essential to get players on the ball as much as possible. The use of small-sided games, restricted areas and rule adaptations were used to develop touch, feel and spatial awareness. Most important, this focus helped to develop players' confidence to accept possession in tight, constricted areas and ability to make better decisions under intense pressure. Some clubs added variety to the learning environment by using different types of balls and allowing players to experience playing on a variety of different surfaces, especially during the early, formative years at 12 and under. In this the clubs are combining messages from the best scientific research (e.g. Ford and Williams, 2011) and practical knowledge derived from coaching. More importantly, this approach is based on the natural play activities of children in unstructured environments. Or, to express it differently, it is guided by the way that generations of children learned the game in Europe before the modern era, and how the game is still learned in many of the poorer parts of the world today.

You tend to find that there is a culture of learning from the base even for the big-name players. For instance, when the research study was carried out, Frank De Boer and Dennis Bergkamp were taking the under-13s and under-14s at Ajax, and Roy Mackay was taking the under-15s at Feyenoord. They were there to learn about coaching and be given a chance to experiment without fear of failure. There tends not to be this type of culture in England, where we often see big-name players finish their playing careers and head straight into management, often without even the basic qualifications. This tends to demoralise others who are trying to progress without the advantage of a high-profile playing career and can undermine the value of learning and qualifications. It also hinders our reputation as a coaching nation around the world, which is reflected in the small number of English coaches working in the top clubs in England and elsewhere. Again, this is being addressed in the EPPP rules, and staff must have the qualifications before they can work in an Academy, not merely be working towards them as was the previous rule.

Generally the players negotiate an individual development plan, which is a great way of maintaining commitment from players and keeping them focused on specific aspects of their game. How much time is devoted to this plan each week did not appear clear, and at some centres it was left to the boy to find the time if it could be undertaken on his own.

The accumulated hours over 10 years do not appear to be significant in that Barcelona were providing only around 3,000 hours of practice time, whereas Aspire were providing nearly 4,700 hours. However, it is also clear that foreign clubs' boys are training more consistently between the age of 12 and 16 with sessions on most days.

These coaching hours prompt a few questions:

- What were they doing before they joined the elite programme that might contribute to their football development?
- What type of practice is going on other than on the grass, and does this count towards Ericsson's 10,000 hour rule?
- How many matches and what type of games per season are the different groups getting?
- What type of coaching methods suit different age groups?
- Are they doing things during school time that might contribute to their football development?
- Is the consistency of being able to train five days per week more important than the actual number of hours?
- As the hours of practice increase, are there significant increases in injury and burnout rates?

The accumulated coaching hours suggest that in football it takes longer to gain the skills necessary to represent the top level teams. This is reflected in the strategy of many foreign clubs to keep players in the system until their early 20s; Zinedine Zidane is a prime example of making his debut in his early 20s in contrast to England, where clubs tend to release players at 18/19 more readily, although the new under-21 league will encourage clubs to hang on to players a little longer and give them more development opportunities.

The coach's role abroad seems more as a facilitator than as the font of all knowledge. The coach sets the practice up with learning outcomes in mind and then lets the session develop, stopping it only occasionally to make a coaching point. So they tended to let the game be the teacher more readily, and this links into Bunker and Thorpe's (1982) Teaching Games for Understanding method. They did step in if the tempo was not to their standard or if any individual seemed not to be concentrating. This suggested that they were more concerned with mental development, although this appeared mainly a subconscious behaviour, as only Ajax had this as a specific outcome to their sessions.

The sessions were consistently 75% or more opposed practices, putting the players into real-life situations where they needed to make decisions and be creative. These ranged from 1 v. 1 all the way up to 11 v. 11 and variations thereof.

It is quite overwhelming from the evidence gathered and the scientific literature that the younger players (6–11) need to learn the game through a player-centred approach that puts them into situations that are game related and lets them try to find the solutions to encourage creativity before guiding them to solutions.

Most clubs have adopted the 1-4-3-3 formation that encourages players to pass the ball through the units, especially the under-12 to under-14 players who may not have the physical ability to play the ball over longer distances and are very much on a steep learning curve regarding their roles and responsibilities within the team.

The games programme for most of the centres actually calls into question the idea of the best playing against the best to develop players to an elite level. They mostly play in regional leagues that sometimes possess only one or two other professional clubs. It was suggested by Gilles Rouillon (Head of Recruitment at AJ Auxerre) that they thought the success in the early years actually helped the boys to maintain their enthusiasm and only when they got older, around 15, did they need to start to play against older boys to get a more competitive environment.

The overriding philosophy of player development as opposed to winning at all costs came through as a common theme, but winning was used in its wider context, and this is summed up by Vince Lombardi (American football coach): "Winning isn't everything but trying to win is."

Education

All the centres have invested time and resources into making sure the boys' educational and pastoral needs are met to facilitate their football development. The best clubs have made arrangements with an educational establishment to work out a diary that suits both parties and allows the boys to have a dual pathway of development. This flexibility has been enjoyed for many years by the foreign clubs but is only recently being exploited by clubs in England through the gifted and talented initiative and the new Academy schools programme. Although clubs have experimented in the past with these types of arrangements (Notts Forest, Arsenal), they all seem to have abandoned them for various reasons. However, Category 1 clubs are now forging links with educational establishments to provide the flexibility in their timetable that provides the coaching time required.

The boys are also supported by part-time tutors to allow them every chance of passing their grades but also to minimise conflict between the club and school. Often, a young player's football development will suffer when he falls behind with his academic work because sanctions usually include stopping the boy from playing or training until he has caught up. The support they get minimises this potential double whammy. However, the 'carrot and stick' approach does work with examples in England at Bolton Wanderers (2000–8), Manchester United's arrangement at Ashton on Mersey School and Bayern Munich.

The merits of hostels or family-based home stays are a much debated topic. Our research revealed that most clubs operate a mix of provision. For instance, AJ Auxerre put all their 16–19 boys into club accommodation but separate the age groups into different buildings. In contrast, Bayern Munich have only a small hostel on site catering for the few foreign boys and those boys from other parts of Germany, as well as some club flats that they allow the 19-plus age group players to use. I feel the universities in England probably get it about right with the first year group staying on-site in University halls of residence to allow the students to be indoctrinated into the culture of the University, and then being pushed out into rented accommodation to fend a little more for themselves. In a football context the second and third year boys would go into home stays, allowing them to switch off from football and enjoy family life. A lot of the Academy Directors expressed their preference for either home stays or travelling from their own homes. With the costs of such a decision in money, time and holistic development, it needs careful planning to decide what will fit each club's situation.

Football in science

Despite the rapid growth in sport science support during the past decade in elite professional football teams, the rate of progress has been much slower in the Academies. This is quite easy to understand from a financial point of view; investment at first team levels tends to come first, and money for youth development is prioritised less at most clubs. Our research and applied experiences suggest that there is something in addition to a lack of resources that has been holding back full acceptance of sport science in the Academies. We believe that there is a commonly held view amongst coaches that sport science would be more effective if it was delivered by football scientists rather than scientists working in football! As one coach at Ajax commented: "the scientific method must be bent to fit the footballer, not the other way around. This means that sport scientists working in youth football should use only what works best, not what is the best science." This was also something we heard many times during our applied work at Bolton in 2001–8. The point they are making, and one we came across frequently elsewhere, is that the application of science to football is the prime concern. To be utilised most effectively, the science will often have to be adapted and used creatively in such a way that it looks less scientific. According to many coaches and medical staff we have encountered, this is a challenge to many sports scientists, especially younger and less experienced ones.

Partly as a result of these reservations about the application of sport science and lack of resources, the provision across the clubs is patchy and inconsistent. For example, performance analysis is an area that has mushroomed in England, including at Academy levels, but has yet to be fully embraced in Europe on a consistent basis. It is an area that can clearly help develop players' tactical and technical development, which could arguably be used towards their accumulated hours of practice. We have seen how skilled and creative sport psychologists have been able to use this data in their work with players to improve emotional control and confidence and enhance self-awareness.

All the Academies visited employed fitness and conditioning specialists or had qualified staff that were able to provide this support. This is a very visible part of development; it is easily measured and therefore not difficult to justify. Many of the staff carrying out this role were also qualified coaches. They were actively involved in coaching alongside their work as fitness or strength and conditioning staff. One of the clearest indications of how valued sport science can become where it is delivered with the strong support of coaches and in a way that meets the demands of youth football is found at Ajax and many other Dutch clubs. The biggest influence of sport science at the Dutch clubs has been the adoption of the Raymond Verheijen Football Fitness Periodisation model. This works on a six-week cycle and is very football-specific, using 4 v. 4, 7 v. 7 and 11 v. 11 games to gauge and improve the fitness levels of the players. Typically used from the age of 13, this is an excellent example of football in science. The science has been adapted to meet the needs of football-specific fitness. Coaches were very enthusiastic about this approach because it worked well, made sense to them and the players, and seemed to be a clear case of sports scientists having thought carefully about the demands of the game first, before finding a solution grounded in science.

In conclusion, the clubs remain quite ambivalent about increasing sport science support at Academy levels. In our confidential dialogue with many key staff, including several with strong scientific backgrounds, we heard repeatedly that the major issue was the scientists and not the science. By this they meant that sport science is being held back from greater acceptance (and effectiveness) because of a failure to educate and train individuals in such a way that their work will be more accepted and valued in football. The criticism levelled at sports scientists is that too often they forget that producing data and information is not their most important task. The key role is to select, interpret and apply their knowledge in such a way that players' performance can be enhanced. This is what their work must be judged against, and not whether it meets the requirements of scientific rigour or established theory. Because this has not always happened in practice, we found many staff who believed that the best way forward for sport science was for this to be delivered more often by coaches. The feeling seemed to be that a new breed of coaching football scientists could help accelerate the acceptance and impact of sport science and overcome the negative perception that strict adherence to the principles of science have often been more important than shaping the science to fit football.

Psychology

Despite hearing often how important this element was in football achievement, we found limited evidence of extensive use of sport psychology at Academy levels. Although it seems this is due to change in England with the introduction of the EPPP, this area remains much underused and rarely delivered by a qualified full-time member of staff on a full-time basis. We have looked at some of the reasons that may explain this; these are easy to understand but more difficult to do something about.

Fundamentally, it seems to come down to coaches not being satisfied with what they have been offered from the sport psychologists who have worked in the game. Dialogue with highly experienced and deep-thinking staff at some of the very best clubs in youth development suggests that they are not expecting psychologists to generate the type of measurable outputs that others sports scientists can provide. They know this is not feasible or desirable. Rather, these coaches accept that the sport psychologist should be assessed in a similar way to themselves; does their presence, knowledge and skill contribute to learning and performance? Specifically, they will need to be convinced that this contribution will be made in a unique way that nevertheless complements the performance enhancement work of the other staff. Without being assured that this will be done, these clubs will continue to be reluctant to bring in staff with expertise in this area. This is despite almost all senior staff without exception claiming that, ultimately, it is the psychological element that differentiates the successful player from the rest, especially at the highest levels of the game.

There was some awareness that some sport psychologists are beginning to advocate the greater use of more natural scientific approaches such as cognitive neuroscience in their work. There is considerable discussion about brain training and anticipation that new and emerging technologies will allow for more focus on the role of neural pathways in learning and performance, for example. Despite this, many of the most experienced staff we have spoken to are concerned that these approaches could make it even harder for coaches and other concerned individuals to resist ideas that make scientific sense but are nonsense when applied to football. Great care will be needed to ensure that the neurological drift in psychology does not detach itself and forget about the person and their mind. As one coach at Feyenoord said to us in a rather pointed way:

> Simple models about brain activity help us to understand more and this is to be welcomed, but the (young) people who learn and play football under our care are incredibly complex human beings. Everything we use is only of use if we keep this in mind at all times!

More positively, there is immense interest in the psychological aspects of football and performance in almost all of the Academies we visited. There is a genuine desire to include this final part of sport science provision more fully into the clubs. However, the research data indicated that clubs wanted the academic sport psychology community to develop an approach to practice that met the needs of young players in elite level football. In summary, this meant placing less emphasis on mental skills training, using player-centred approaches more often and encouraging the psychologists and coaches to draw on perspectives that challenge individuals to find their own solutions to problems.

Governance

To conclude, it is clear that there is strong leadership within the national associations and club environments with a clear vision of what they want to produce and how to do that. This joined-up thinking binds the clubs and national centres together for the common good, and with France being the most productive of professional footballers inside the EU playing in the top five leagues in Europe, they seem to be doing something right. Also, the 2010 World Cup final was contested by Spain and Holland, with eight players in both squads developed by Barcelona and Ajax, respectively. Germany, alongside France, now boasts the youngest squads in the top five leagues in Europe at their Bundesliga and Liga 1 clubs, with an average age of 25.4. This is obviously providing opportunities to their young players that are creating the platform for club and international success.

Based on the research and our applied experiences, we would make the following 15 major recommendations:

1 Countries that are led by their governing body in the area of youth development are able to make necessary changes a lot quicker and align critical parts of the process for the betterment of the national team first, which also has a positive knock-on effect for clubs.
2 There should be a common vision and philosophy running through the whole club, from first team to Academy. This is the case at most of the clubs we visited, and especially at Barcelona, Ajax and Bayern Munich.
3 Realistic and consistent budgets need to be ring-fenced to ensure financial stability and long-term investment – so that clubs see their Academy as a profit centre and not a cost centre.
4 Many of the successful Academies and national centres benefit from high levels of staff consistency. This is partly due to the management structure and reporting lines, i.e. the Academy Manager reports directly to the board, not the first team manager. Retaining Academy staff despite changes in first team environments is vital for continuity of care and stability.
5 In terms of talent identification, the new EPPP regulation in England will allow clubs to recruit players nationally from the age of 12 from the 2013/14 season. This is in line with many other European countries. This will benefit clubs, national teams and individual player progression.
6 Holistic screening processes should be carried out from age under-14 onwards to reduce risk and increase success rates.
7 Same-site training grounds provides for better cohesion and consistency, as well as development. All of the clubs visited around Europe operated from one site; this should be an aspiration for all clubs, irrespective of size.
8 Across some of the most successful clubs in the world, many famous and former senior players work with young players in the Academy as they learn their craft. More staff should expect to start their coaching and work in football at youth levels before moving on to senior levels.
9 Increased use of individual development plans is needed to accelerate learning and achievement. An outstanding example of this to follow is at Ajax. They have chosen to invest extra resources into their top four players from under-14 onwards.
10 Training hours do not appear to reach anywhere near the 10,000 hour rule. More importantly, training takes place on most days and in a manner that challenges and stretches players. Technical programs are used creatively as a guide for the coaches, and not as a prescriptive tool. Players should be encouraged to

play informal, self-directed and unstructured fun sessions within and/or away from the training ground to hone skills and build football-related fitness.

11 Clubs must allow players to learn the game through playing the game. Game-related, opposed practice sessions dominated, with a ratio approximately of 25% unopposed to 75% opposed.

12 Most teams played a variation of 1-4-3-3, as this encourages a possession-based game with shorter passing and more creativity.

13 All the clubs visited embraced the Lombardi ethos to development: "winning isn't everything but trying to win is!"

14 Education and welfare needs were addressed as part of the moral contract; there was no question of compromise, in comparison to England, where it has taken the EPPP to force clubs to address this fundamental need fully and consistently.

15 In terms of accommodation needs, the best models involve using an approach similar to what the Universities have been doing for many years: players would be expected to live in home stays, but only after living the first year on-site.

REFERENCES

Abraham, A., and Collins, D. (2011). Taking the next step: New directions for coaching science. *Quest* 6, 366–384.

Andersen, M. B. (2005). Yeah, I work with Beckham: Issues of confidentiality, privacy and privilege in sport psychology service delivery. *Sport and Exercise Psychology Review* 1, 5–13.

Andersen, M. B. (2009). Performance enhancement as a bad start and a dead end: A parenthetical comment on Mellalieu and Lane. *The Sport and Exercise Scientist* 20, 12–14.

Andersen, M. B., and Tod, D. (2006). When to refer athletes for counselling or psychotherapy. In J. M. Williams (ed.), *Applied Sport Psychology: Personal Growth to Peak Performance*. Boston: McGraw-Hill, pp. 483–495.

Anderson, A. G., Miles, A., Robinson, P., and Mahoney, C. (2004). Evaluating the athlete's perception of the sport psychologist's effectiveness: What should we be assessing? *Psychology of Sport and Exercise* 5, 255–277.

Balague, G. (1999). Understanding identity, value and meaning when working with elite athletes. *The Sport Psychologist* 13, 89–98.

Bishop, D. (2010). Dietary supplements and team performance. *Sports Medicine* 40, 995–1017.

Bloom, B. S. (1985). *Developing Talent in Young People*. New York: Ballantine.

Bloom, B. S., Engelhart, M. D., Furst, E. J., Hill, W. H., and Krathwohl D. R. (1956). *Taxonomy of Educational Objectives*. London: Longmans.

Bota, J. (1993). Development of the Ottawa mental skills Assessment tool. University of Ottawa.

Brady, A., and Maynard, I. (2010). At an elite level the role of the sport psychologist is entirely about performance enhancement. *Sport and Exercise Psychology Review* 6, 59–66.

Brady, C., Bolchover, D., and Sturgess, B. (2008). Managing in the talent economy: The football model for business. *California Management Review* 50, 54–73.

Brown, G., and Potrac, P. (2009). 'You've not made the grade, son': De-selection and identity disruption in elite level youth football. *Soccer and Society* 10, 143–159.

Bunker, D., and Thorpe, R. (1982). A model for the teaching of games in secondary schools. *Bulletin of Physical Education*.

Chelladurai, P., and Trail, G. (2006). Styles of decision making in coaching. In J. M. Williams (ed.), *Applied Sport Psychology: Personal Growth to Peak Performance*. Boston: McGraw-Hill, pp. 107–119.

Collins, J. (2001). *Good to Great*. Random House: London.

Cook, C., Crust, L., Littlewood, M., Nesti, M., and Allen-Collinson, J. (2014). 'What it takes': Perceptions of mental toughness and its development in an English Premier League Soccer Academy. *Qualitative Research in Sport, Exercise and Health* 6, 329–347.

Cook, M. (2006). *Soccer Coaching: The Professional Way*. London: A & C Black.

Corlett, J. (1996a). Sophistry, Socrates and sport psychology. *The Sport Psychologist* 10, 84–94.

Corlett, J. (1996b). Virtue lost: Courage in sport. *Journal of the Philosophy of Sport* 23, 45–57.

Covey, S. (1989). *The 7 Habits of Highly Effective People*. New York: Simon & Schuster.

Cruickshank, A., Collins, D., and Minten, S. (2014). Driving and sustaining culture change in Olympic sport performance teams: A first exploration and grounded theory. *Journal of Sport & Exercise Psychology* 36, 107–120.

Crust, L. (2007). Mental toughness in sport: A review. *International Journal of Sport and Exercise Psychology* 5, 270–290.

Csikszentmihalyi, M. (1996). *Flow and the Psychology of Discovery and Invention*. New York: Harper Perennial.

Cumming, J. and Hall, C. (2002). Deliberate imagery practice: the development of imagery skills in competitive athletes. *Journal of Sports Sciences* 2, 137–145.

Deci, E. L., and Ryan, R. M. (1985). *Intrinsic Motivation and Self-Determination in Human Behaviour*. New York: Plenum Press.

Drust, D., Reilly, T., and Williams, A. M. (2009). *International Research in Science and Soccer: The Proceedings of the First World Conference on Science and Soccer*. London: Routledge.

Elliott, R., and Weedon, G. (2010). Foreign players in the English Premier Academy League: 'Feet-drain' or 'feet-exchange'. *International Review for the Sociology of Sport* 46, 61–75.

Ericsson, K. A. (1993). The development of elite performance and deliberate practice: An update from the perspective of the expert-performance approach. In J. Starkes and K. A. Ericsson (eds.), *Expert Performance in Sport: Recent Advances in Research on Sport Expertise*. Champaign IL: Human Kinetics, pp. 49–81.

Fairhurst, G. T. (2008). Discursive leadership: A communication alternative to leadership psychology. *Management Communication Quarterly* 21, 510–521.

Fforde, M. (2009). *Desocialisation: The Crisis of Post-Modernity*. Cheadle Hume: Gabriel.

Fletcher, D., and Wagstaff, C. R. D. (2009). Organizational psychology in elite sport: Its emergence, application and future. *Psychology of Sport and Exercise* 10, 427–434.

Ford, P. R., and Williams, A. M. (2011). The developmental activities engaged in by the elite youth soccer players who progressed to professional status compared to those who did not. *Psychology of Sport and Exercise* 13, 349–352.

Gilbourne, D., and Richardson, D. (2006). Tales from the field: Personal reflections on the provision of psychological support in professional soccer. *Psychology of Sport and Exercise* 7, 335–337.

Gilmore, S. E., and Gilson, C. H. J. (2007). Finding form: Elite sports and the business of change. *Journal of Organization Change Management* 20, 409–423.

Gilson, C., Pratt, M., Roberts, K., and Weymes, E. (2001). *Peak Performance: Business Lessons from the World's Top Sports Organisations*. London: Harper Collins.

Giorgi, A. (1970). *Psychology as a Human Science*. New York: Harper and Row.

Gladwell, M. (2008). *Outliers*. London: Penguin.

Gould, D. (2001). *Goal Setting for Peak Performance*. Greensboro: University of North Carolina.

Jackson, S., and Csikszentmihalyi, M. (1999). *Flow in Sports*. Champaign, IL: Human Kinetics.

Jones, G. (1995). More than just a game: Research developments and issues in competitive anxiety in sport. *British Journal of Psychology* 86, 449–478.

Kuhn, T. (1977). *The Essential Tension: Selected Studies in Scientific Tradition and Change*. Chicago: University of Chicago Press.

Kuhn, T., and Jackson, M. (2008). Accomplishing knowledge: A framework for investigating knowing in organizations. *Management Communication Quarterly* 21, 454–485.

Lewis, M. (2003). *Moneyball: The Art of Winning an Unfair Game.* New York: W. W. Norton.

Littlewood, M. (2005). The impact of foreign player acquisition on the development and progression of young players in elite level English professional football. Unpublished PhD thesis, Liverpool John Moores University, UK.

Littlewood, M., Mullen, C., and Richardson, D. (2011). Football labour migration: An examination of the player recruitment strategies of the 'big five' European football leagues 2004–5 to 2008–9. *Soccer & Society* 12, 788–805.

Maddi, S. R. (2004). Hardiness: An operationalisation of existential courage. *Journal of Humanistic Psychology* 44, 360–368.

Magee, J. (2002). Shifting balances of power in the new football economy. In J. Sugden (ed.), *Power Games: A Critical Sociology of Sport.* London: Routledge.

Maslow, A. H. (1968). *Toward a Psychology of Being.* New York: Van Nostrand Reinhold Company.

May, R. (1975). *The Courage to Create.* New York: Norton.

May, R. (1977). *The Meaning of Anxiety.* New York: Ronald Press.

Mitchell, T., Nesti, M., Richardson, D., Midgeley, A. W., Eubank, M., and Littlewood, M. (2014). Exploring athletic identity in elite level English youth football: A cross sectional approach. *Journal of Sports Sciences* 32, 1294–1299.

Murray, M. C., and Mann, B. L. (2001). Leadership effectiveness. In J. M. Williams (ed.), *Applied Sport Psychology: Personal Growth to Peak Performance.* Boston: McGraw-Hill, pp. 83–106.

Nakamura M., Sakakibara, S., and Schroder, R. (1998). Adoption of Just-in-Time manufacturing methods at U.S.- and Japanese-owned plants: Some empirical evidence. *IEEE Trans Engineering Management* 45, 230–240.

Nele, M., Sayer, C., and Pinto, J. C. (1999). Computation of molecular weight distributions by polynomial approximation with complete adaptation procedures. *Macromolecular Theory and Simulations* 8, 199–213.

Nesti, M. (2004). *Existential Psychology and Sport: Theory and Application.* London: Routledge.

Nesti, M. (2010). *Psychology in Football: Working with Elite and Professional Players.* London: Routledge.

Nesti, M. S. (2007). Persons and players. In J. Parry, M. S. Nesti, S. Robinson, and N. Watson (eds.), *Sport and Spirituality: An Introduction.* London: Routledge, pp. 135–150.

Nesti, M., and Littlewood, M. (2009). Psychological preparation and development of players in premiership football: Practical and theoretical perspectives. In T. Riley., A. M. Williams, and B. Drust (eds.), *International Research in Science and Soccer.* London: Routledge, pp. 169–176.

Nesti, M., and Littlewood, M. (2011). Making your way in the game: Boundary situations within the world of professional football. In D. Gilbourne and M. Andersen (eds.), *Critical Essays in Sport Psychology.* Champaign, IL: Human Kinetics, pp. 233–250.

Nesti, M., Littlewood, M., O'Halloran, L., Eubank, M., and Richardson, D. (2012). Critical moments in elite premiership football: Who do you think you are? *Physical Culture and Sport Studies and Research* 56, 23–32.

Orlick, T. (2000). *In Pursuit of Excellence: How to Win in Sport and Life Through Mental Training.* Champaign, IL: Human Kinetics.

Pain, M., and Harwood, C. (2007). The performance environment of the England youth soccer teams. *Journal of Sports Sciences* 25, 1307–1324.

Parker, A. (1995). Great expectations: Grimness or glamour? The football apprentice in the 1990s. *The Sports Historian* 15, 107–126.

Ravizza, K. (2002). A philosophical construct: A framework for performance enhancement. *International Journal of Sport Psychology* 33, 4–18.

Reilly, T., Williams, A. M., Nevill, A., and Franks, M. (2000). A multidisciplinary approach to talent identification in soccer. *Journal of Sport Sciences* 18, 668–676.

Relvas, H., Littlewood, M., Nesti, M., Gilbourne, D., and Richardson, D. (2010). Organisational structures and working practices in elite European professional football clubs. *European Sport Management Quarterly* 10, 165–187.

Richardson, D., Gilbourne, D., and Littlewood, M. (2004). Developing support mechanisms for elite young players in a professional soccer academy. *European Sport Management Quarterly* 4, 195–214.

Roderick, M. (2006). *The Work of Professional Football: A Labour of Love.* London: Routledge.

Selye, H. (1956). *The Stress of Life.* New York: McGraw-Hill.

Simonton, D. K. (2001). Talent development as a multidimensional, multiplicative, and dynamic process. *Current Directions in Psychological Science* 10, 39–43.

Smith, R. E., and Christensen, D. S. (1995). Psychological skills as predictors of performance and survival in professional baseball. *Journal of Sport and Exercise Psychology* 17, 399–415.

Stratton, G., Reilly, T., Williams, A. M., and Richardson, D. (2004). *Youth Soccer: From Science to Performance.* London: Routledge.

Svensson, M., and Drust, B. (2005). Testing soccer players. *Journal of Sports Science* 23, 601–618.

The Premier League. (2011). *Elite Player Performance Plan May 2011.* London: Premier League.

Van Yperen, N. W. (2009). Why some make it and others do not: Identifying psychological factors that predict career success in professional adult soccer. *The Sport Psychologist* 23, 317–329.

Williams, J. M. (ed.) (2006). *Applied Sport Psychology: Personal Growth to Peak Performance.* Boston: McGraw-Hill.

Williams, M. (ed.) (2013). *Science and Soccer: Developing Elite Performers.* London: Routledge.

Wilson, A. M. (2001). Understanding organisational culture and the implications for corporate marketing. *European Journal of Marketing* 35, 353–367.

INDEX